RIPPED

1953—age 15.

1962—age 24.

1968—age 30.

1979—age 41. *Photo by Bill Reynolds.*

RIPPED

The Sensible Way to Achieve Ultimate Muscularity.

by Clarence Bass

Mr. America Past 40, Short Class (1978)

Mr. U.S.A. Past 40, Short Class (1979)

Best Abdominals, Mr. U.S.A. Past 40 (1979)

Best Legs, Mr. U.S.A. Past 40 (1979)

Most Muscular Man, Mr. U.S.A. Past 40 (1979)

Clarence Bass' Ripped Enterprises
Albuquerque, New Mexico

ISBN–13: 978–0–9609714–0–4
ISBN–10: 0–9609714–0–8

Other Books by Clarence Bass:

RIPPED 2
The all-new companion volume to Ripped

RIPPED 3
The Recipes, The Routines and The Reasons

THE LEAN ADVANTAGE
Four years of the Ripped Question and Answer Department

THE LEAN ADVANTAGE 2
The Second Four Years

THE LEAN ADVANTAGE 3
Four More Years

LEAN FOR LIFE
The Lifestyle Approach to Leanness

CHALLENGE YOURSELF
Leanness, Fitness & Health at any age

Twelfth Printing 2014

Published by Clarence Bass' Ripped Enterprises
P.O. Box 51236
Albuquerque, New Mexico 87181-1236 USA

RIPPED ™ is the trademark of Clarence and Carol Bass.

Library of Congress Catalog card number: 80–81446
ISBN–13: 978–0–9609714–0–4
ISBN–10: 0–9609714–0–8

Front and back cover photos by Bill Reynolds.

*To my father
who kindled my first interest
in strength and exercise
and
who has encouraged me always.*

ACKNOWLEDGMENTS

I am deeply grateful to Dr. Ulrich C. Luft, his staff, and Lovelace Medical Center for their cheerful and unsparing assistance. Without their help this book would not be possible.

My thanks also to Sharon Clark and Marcia Mazria for their dedicated and enthusiastic editing assistance.

CONTENTS

INTRODUCTION

At the 1979 Past 40 Mr. U.S.A. contest, I won the Best Abdominals, Best Legs, and the Most Muscular Man awards. Ralph Countryman, head of the AAU Physique Judges Committee, said that I was more than "cut": I was "etched." After years of training, I finally hit my stride and chalked up a major national level victory.

In 1954 I received my first trophy, for winning the New Mexico State High School Pentathlon Championship, a five event contest made up of pushups, chinups, jump reach, bar vault, and the 300-yard shuttle run. In the following years I won many trophies in Olympic and Power lifting. I became an avid runner and bicyclist, and I developed a deep, active interest in nutrition and overall body fitness. I am a practicing lawyer; I'm married, and I have a wonderful seven year old son, but I've never lost my interest in strength and muscle building. I'm more interested in muscle building now, at age 41, than ever before.

Twenty-six years ago I saw Bill Pearl win the Mr. America title, but it wasn't until I saw Vic Seipke win the 1976 Past 40 Mr. America title that I decided to enter bodybuilding competition myself. I saw Vic win the 1955 Jr. Mr. America when I competed in the Junior National Olympic Lift Championship, and I was one of the judges at the 1976 Past 40 Mr. America competition, where he became the first AAU National Master's Physique Champion. I was thrilled to see Vic looking as good in 1976 as he did in 1955. Inspired by Seipke's success, I decided that I, too, could be a National Master's physique champion.

This book tells you what I've learned through almost three decades of weight training, and how I used that knowledge to become a physique champion. Whether you're interested in attaining the "etched" condition I achieved, or you simply want a leaner, more muscular physique, this book will show you the way.

Ripped focuses on the years 1977 through 1979, detailing what I did to achieve ultra lean condition each year. By examining what I did right, and just as important, what I did wrong, I explain the sensible way to achieve ultimate muscularity. As I write this in September 1979, less than two months before my 42nd birthday, I have the best physique I've ever had. I will be better in 1980 and the years that follow. I'm convinced this book will help *you* become leaner, harder, and more muscular — better next year and in the years that follow.

PART ONE

24% Body Fat

July 1977, shortly before the first body composition test. Body fat: 2.4%.
Photo by Dave Sauer.

1977 was a preparation year:
I created the best diet for maximum definition
and I reached ultraleanness,
but I overtrained and sacrificed muscle tissue.

The First Step

In 1973 Arthur Jones was the talk of the bodybuilding world. His Nautilus machines were going to develop muscles of superhuman size and strength. My wife, Carol, and I went to Florida to talk to Arthur about his muscle and strength building theories. We talked to him for hours on end over two days. He doesn't pull any punches. One of the things he told me was that I needed to lose 20 pounds. I was shocked! I weighed about 175 lbs., and I thought I was in pretty good shape. Arthur recommended that I first reduce my body fat to a minimum level and only then attempt to gain muscle. He explained that it's very difficult to gain muscle and lose fat at the same time. He also said the practice of gaining muscle and fat, bulking up, and then reducing is wrong, because you end up right where you started: The muscle comes off with the fat.

Arthur's advice stuck with me. It made sense. In late 1976 I began planning my entry into past 40 bodybuilding competition and I decided that the first step was to reduce to fat-free condition. The problem was there were many different diets, all claiming to be the best. I had to discover the diet that was *the best!*

3

The Diet Maze

Over the years I had read most of the best known books on diet including Dr. Atkins' book on the high protein, high fat, low carbohydrate diet. I had tried Dr. Atkins' diet and I remember how terrible I felt. I was tired, shaky, and irritable; I felt deprived and unsatisfied. That type of diet was definitely not for me. Dr. Atkins' book, and a book called *Sweet and Dangerous* by John Yudkin, M.D. on the evils of sugar, had, however, convinced me that highly processed, concentrated carbohydrate foods should be avoided. I had also read Dr. David Reuben's book, *The Save Your Life Diet,* which extolled the virtues of the high fiber diet, and *Did You Ever See a Fat Squirrel?* by Ruth Adams. Ruth Adams wrote convincingly that if you make it a lifetime habit to eat only natural, unprocessed foods, you'll never be overweight and you'll never be hungry or feel deprived. Influenced by Drs. Atkins, Yudkin, and Reuben, and especially by Ruth Adams, I planned the diet I hoped would take me to a fat-free condition.

After wrestling my way through the maze of diet and nutrition books, I decided my diet should be high in natural, unprocessed foods, and extremely low in concentrated calorie foods.

The diet I created succeeded beyond my wildest dreams.

Results in Perspective

There are two kinds of body fat: "essential fat," necessary for good health, and "storage fat," the kind of fat you want to lose. Essential fat surrounds and protects the internal organs, like the heart, liver, kidneys, and the spleen, and it's indispensable to the functioning of brain and nerve tissue.

The average male has a body fat level of 15 per cent. Kyle Rote Jr., professional soccer player and hero of the "Superstars" TV program has been measured at 10.2% body fat. Top quality marathon runners carry five to six per cent body fat. Exercise physiologists put the rock bottom essential fat level in males at

3%. Even in starvation, the essential fat level drops only slightly, because the body fights to keep its vital organ systems functioning properly. A body fat level of 3% or lower is, in effect, "zero" fat.*

When my body fat was measured at Lovelace Medical Center on August 24, 1977, I knew the diet I planned and followed was amazingly successful. My body fat level was 2.4%!

Dieting Without Suffering

I reduced my body fat level to 2.4% without starving, without hunger, and without feeling deprived in any way. Hunger and deprivation don't have to be a part of dieting.

A diet is much more likely to be successful if you can live with it comfortably. The conventional low calorie and low carbohydrate diets work, but they usually don't work on a long term basis, because they leave you hungry or feeling deprived.

Your family doctor may say to you, "Eat everything you normally eat, just eat a little less than you do now and you will lose weight." I don't believe this is practical. If you follow that advice, you *will* lose weight, but you'll have a hard time doing it; you'll be hungry.

Most bodybuilders, including the superstars, use low or zero carbohydrate diets to reach contest condition. I think this is a mistake. You may not be hungry on the low carbohydrate diet, but you will feel deprived; you'll crave carbohydrate foods.

The diet I followed in 1977 is superior to the conventional low calorie diet and the low carbohydrate diet: It's both filling *and* satisfying.

---

*The information I present on body fat levels has been provided by Ulrich C. Luft, M.D., Head of the Department of Physiology at Lovelace Medical Center in Albuquerque, New Mexico, and Bill Penner, *Iron Man* magazine contributing author. For more information read "All About Body Fat" by James C. G. Coniff in the October 1978 issue of *The Runner* magazine. Mr. Coniff's article is based on an interview with Dr. William D. McArdle, exercise physiologist at New York's Queens College. Dr. McArdle is an expert on body fat and its role in the functioning of the human body. He is also co-author of the book, *Nutrition, Weight Control and Exercise* (Houghton Mifflin 1977).

LOVELACE FOUNDATION FOR MEDICAL EDUCATION AND RESEARCH

5200 Gibson Boulevard, Southeast   Albuquerque, New Mexico 87108   Phone 842-7171

DEPARTMENT OF
PHYSIOLOGY

August 26, 1977

Clarence R. Bass
305 Sandia Savings Building
400 Gold SW
Albuquerque, NM   87102

Dear Mr. Bass:

Here are the results of the measurements of body composition we made on
you a few days ago. I have also added the results of your exercise test in June
for your records.

<u>Body Composition</u> August 24, 1977

Gross Weight: 70.60 kg (155 lbs, 11 oz)

Fat: 1.69 kg (2.4% of Gr. W.)

Lean Body Mass: 68.91 kg

The average normal fat content for your age group is 15.7%.

<u>Maximal Capacity Exercise</u> June 9, 1977

Maximal Oxygen Uptake: 3.572 liter/min

Maximal Power Output: 1725 m·kg/min

Maximal Heart Rate: 180/min

Average max. oxygen uptake for a man of your age and
weight is 2.379 liters/min. Thus you are 50% above average.

Give me a call some time in the latter part of October and we will give you an
appointment for another weighing.

Yours sincerely,

Ulrich C. Luft, M.D.
Head, Department of Physiology

UCL/djr

Concentrated Calories

Avoid concentrated calories: That is my cardinal rule! For example, sugar contains calories in one of the most concentrated forms. On the other hand, the apple has a great deal of volume, with a low concentration of calories. When you eat all of the sugar, or all of the sugar filled foods you want, you take in more calories than your body can use and you become fat. By contrast, you can gorge yourself on apples and you won't take in more calories than your body can use and you won't become fat. Butter is another good example of a concentrated calorie food, while the potato, like the apple, has a low concentration of calories. You can eat your fill of plain baked potato and not get fat, but if you drench your potato in butter you will get fat.

Concentrated calorie foods also stimulate the appetite and encourage you to overeat. You eat more baked potato when you add butter than if you eat it plain. The food processers know exactly what they're doing when they add sugar to processed foods. The more sugar they add, the more you eat, the more they sell, and the fatter you become.

The formula for losing weight is no secret: eat fewer calories than you burn up. Self discipline is the problem: It's hard to discipline yourself to eat fewer calories than you burn up. I found the solution to this problem. I discovered by eating only natural, unprocessed foods, you avoid almost all concentrated calorie foods, and you won't overeat. You'll become lean.

My Diet

For breakfast I ate a cereal I made myself with the following ingredients: rolled oats, unprocessed coarse wheat bran, wheat germ, sunflower seeds, raisins or other dried fruit, and grade A whole raw milk. Rolled oats and bran made up the major portion of the cereal because they are high in fiber and bulk and low in calories. The other ingredients, especially the sunflower seeds and the dried fruit, (concentrated calorie foods), were used sparingly. This cereal is nourishing, filling, and tastes good. It's low in calories because, with the exception of the sunflower seeds and the dried fruit, it contains no concentrated calorie foods. In particular, it contains none of the concentrated calorie foods usually found in cereals, even those sold in health food stores: honey, syrup, molasses, raw sugar, and oil.

Lunch was a problem because I had to take it with me to the office. I had a peanut butter sandwich, one cup of raw milk or yogurt, and an apple or plain baked potato. Since regular supermarket peanut butter is almost always filled with sugar, the peanut butter I used was made of peanuts and nothing else. It contained no sugar and no salt. (I never add salt to anything.) You can find this type of peanut butter in most health food stores or you can make your own at home. I used whole grain bread from a health food store. I read the labels on the bread for ingredients and calories per serving and picked the lowest calorie whole grain bread I could find. Sometimes my wife made the bread at home so we could completely control the ingredients. This is preferable because even the whole grain bread sold in health food stores contains honey or other concentrated calories.

My evening meal was a salad made with assorted greens, raw fresh vegetables, eggs, and a few nuts. Using your imagination you can create a huge, delicious, nourishing, and filling salad, still low in calories. My favorite ingredients are cabbage, (sweeter and crunchier than lettuce), collard greens, spinach, broccoli, cauliflower, carrots, tomatoes, bell peppers, onions, radishes, sprouts, cucumbers, squash, and fresh green beans. But beware of the dressing. Dressing contains oil and, usually, sugar. It's like the butter on the baked potato. In addition to adding calories it tends to make you eat more than you would ordinarily to feel full and satisfied. You'll find the type of salad I have described tastes delicious with no dressing at all. If I used any dressing at all, it was vinegar and pepper. You could also use herbs like sage, tarragon, oregano, and rosemary. I used no oil. (One tablespoon of corn oil contains as many calories as two ears of corn on the cob and I would much prefer to eat two ears of corn!) If I was hungry later in the evening I had fresh fruit, usually apples or pears. I ate the skin and the seeds, everything but the stem.

In 1977 I didn't count calories, nonetheless my diet was

low in calories. I weighed myself in the morning, every day, before breakfast. Because your weight will vary during the day, it's important to weigh yourself at the same time, every day. My weight gradually kept going down until the mirror told me I was quite lean. I didn't rush the reducing process. I took from January until July 1977 to lose approximately ten pounds. By losing slowly I didn't have to drastically reduce my food intake, I was never hungry, and I never craved other foods. In 1979 I had to cut calories more to lose faster. This diet did the job and did it painlessly.

Uniformity Makes It Easy

My diet was made up of foods I enjoyed and I ate basically the same thing every day. I know eating the same thing every day may not appeal to some of you. I still recommend you follow the same basic menu every day. If you eat different things every day you won't know how many calories you are taking in and it's harder to maintain the fat burning process. By keeping my meals uniform I was able to control the number of calories I ate and maintain the fat burning process, without counting calories. When my weight levelled off I adjusted the diet slightly until it started down again by simply decreasing portions or subtracting food items. For example, to reduce calories in the cereal you can put in more bran and cut down the other ingredients which are higher in calories. Twelve tablespoons of bran contain only 200 calories. A lower calorie version of the cereal mixture I sometimes use is:

    2 tablespoons wheat germ
    5 tablespoons bran
    1 tablespoon sunflower seeds
    1 tablespoon raisins
    1 cup whole milk

To reduce calories even further leave out the sunflower seeds and/or the raisins. Without the nuts or dried fruit, this cereal mixture still has a nice sweet taste from the milk.For lunch you can reduce the amount of peanut butter in the sandwich or omit the apple or potato. With practice, you can easily master this adjustment process.

Do I Have To Eat the Same Thing Every Day?

If you still want to vary your diet go ahead. You will, however, have to spend more time in planning your daily menu.

Become a label reader. Everything in a box, package, bottle, or can usually has the fiber and bulk removed and sugar added. Junk foods are the worst examples of the concentrated calorie foods. Whenever possible eat foods in their natural state with the fiber and bulk still in them and with nothing added. Whole grains, fresh fruits, and vegetables should make up a major portion of your diet. Eat fruits and vegetables with the skin left on. I eat the seeds too. Avoid fruit or vegetable juices because all the natural fiber and bulk have been removed. This increases the calorie concentration. Eat the fruit or vegetables instead. Eat plenty of foods that are large in bulk and low in calories. These are filling and satisfying, but not fattening. Emphasize natural, unprocessed, whole, high fiber foods and avoid concentrated calorie foods. Keep your eyes on the scale and the mirror.

When you're under pressure to trim down fat before a contest, a picture taking session, or some other important date, you'll need a calorie counter book to gauge your reduction more precisely. I use *Calories and Carbohydrates,* an excellent guide by Barbara Kraus.

The Milk Myth

You may be surprised I included milk and yogurt in my reducing diet. It's true some people can't digest milk. (Those with this problem may find they can tolerate yogurt.) Milk is one of the most nutritious and balanced foods. If you can digest milk, there's no reason to exclude it from a reducing diet. Many people in bodybuilding say milk makes you smooth. Milk, in moderation, won't make you smooth. Excess calories add fat and make you smooth, not any specific food. Top Mr. Olympia contender, Mike Mentzer, even eats ice cream while cutting up for a contest. Ice cream stimulates your appetite and I think eating it regularly is asking for trouble; but milk is OK. Don't accept bodybuilding myths at face value. Except for a brief period in 1978, I've always included milk in my diet and it hasn't made me smooth.

No Meat, Fish, or Chicken?

My diet doesn't include the mainstays of the most commonly used definition diets: meat, fish, and chicken. The protein in eggs and milk is better balanced and more usable than the protein in meat, fish, or chicken. However, the main reason I exclude these foods is they don't contain fiber and they slow down the digestion process. The digestion and elimination process is faster if meat, fish, and chicken are not included in the diet. Meat, fish, and chicken make me constipated. Check it out on yourself. Eat no meat, fish, or chicken for a week, then put them back in your diet. You'll notice a definite difference in your bowel movements. When I occasionally eat these foods in a restaurant my weight goes up and I feel a fullness for several days.

A complete discussion of the advantages of faster digestion and elimination is found in Dr. Reuben's book, *The Save Your Life Diet.* The advantages of the high fiber diet go far beyond the control of obesity.

The Protein Requirement

I've believed in a high protein diet all my life, but recently I changed my mind. I urge you to read the discussion of the body's need for protein in Nathan Pritikin's new book, *The Pritikin Program for Diet & Exercise,* and in Robin Hur's lesser known, but well researched book, *Food Reform.** It's sobering to read Pritikin's and Hur's condemnation of the high protein diet. They conclude excessive protein is harmful, because it causes a loss of bone calcium which can weaken the bones, and it also causes a rise in uric acid levels creating a risk of gout. Most high protein foods would be more accurately classified as high fat foods and there is evidence they contribute to obesity, cut down endurance, and shorten the life span.

My diet contains only a moderate amount of protein, mainly from eggs, milk, and nuts. Another bodybuilding myth maintains you need massive quantities of protein. I believe the protein requirement has been grossly overstated by many of the experts in the health food field, and especially in the bodybuilding field. My diet contains adequate protein particularly since it includes plenty of carbohydrates for energy. If you don't eat enough carbohydrates, your body is forced to use protein to supply energy. By meeting my energy requirements through carbohydrate foods, my need for protein is reduced. Since the

*Food Reform, (Heidelberg Publishers 1975), is available from Vegetarian Resource, 2455 Calle Roble, Thousand Oaks, California 91360.

protein in my diet is not called upon to supply energy, it's available to fulfill its primary functions: maintenance, repair, and growth of body tissue.

If you want to measure your protein intake, the standard recommendation of one gram of protein for every 2.2 pounds (one kilogram) of bodyweight is enough. I don't count grams of protein, but I do make it a point to include good quality protein foods like eggs, milk, or yogurt with each of my main meals.

Supplements

I won't dwell on vitamin and mineral supplementation, because my diet is well balanced. It draws heavily from each of the four major food groups: the meat or egg group, the milk group, the bread and cereal group, and the fruit and vegetable group. Supplementation isn't as necessary with my balanced diet as it is with an unbalanced diet like the low carbohydrate diet. As a protective measure, I do, however, take a high potency multiple vitamin and mineral supplement. I also take additional Vitamin C to aid tissue repair, Vitamin E to promote better blood circulation, and the B Complex vitamins to protect against stress and aid protein metabolism. A discussion of the need for vitamin and mineral supplements is beyond the scope of this book. If you're interested in that area I urge you to read Richard Passwater's two books, *Supernutrition* and *Supernutrition for Healthy Hearts*. As a vitamin and mineral reference book, I recommend *Mental and Elemental Nutrients* by Carl C. Pfeiffer, Ph.D., M.D. In addition, I subscribe to *Prevention* magazine, and I suggest that you do too.

Eating Out

A diet problem we all face from time to time is eating out. I follow a few basic rules which allow me to enjoy myself without interfering with my training goals. Frequently I find a salad on the menu, or better yet, a salad bar, which gives me very nearly the same huge, delicious, filling, and nutritious salad I make at home. If the salad bar selection offers a rich variety, I often have the salad as my main course. At most good restaurants salads are now "in." People have become diet conscious and many are interested in vegetarianism. In response, many restaurants offer delicious vegetable plates, in addition to the salad bar. I order vinegar as dressing for my salad. I order whole wheat toast, unbuttered. I specify I want my baked potato dry, with no butter, and no sour cream. Many restaurants now serve omelettes at any time of day. I particularly like mushroom or spinach omelette, but I avoid the traditional ham and cheese.

I sometimes find, however, that steak, fish, or chicken are the most acceptable items on the menu. If this is the case I choose fish or chicken over steak. Fish and chicken have less fat than steak so they're lower in calories. With no alternative but steak, I order it lean and rare. Obviously lean steak has fewer calories, and it's easier to digest if it's cooked rare. I like chopped sirloin because chopped meat has a head start on the digestion process. I would not order anything fried because fried foods contain too many concentrated calories. I skip sauces for the same reason.

The real danger item on the menu is dessert. Dessert makes me hungrier since concentrated calorie foods stimulate the appetite. A cup of good coffee with cream and an artificial sweetener is more satisfying. If you must have dessert (on occasion I can't resist either), then a restaurant is the best place to have it. There you'll probably stop at one dessert even if you secretly would like to have a second one. At home, it's too easy to have a second or even third helping of dessert. There, the best rule on desserts is, "Absolutely Not." If you're like me, it's hard to stop with one dessert. At home, my seven year old son watches his dessert like a hawk. I watch it too!

At the recent week long National Amateur Athletic Union convention in Las Vegas, Nevada, I didn't gain an ounce. In fact, by following my "eating out rules" I lost one and one-eighth pounds. At the Sultan's table in The Dunes Hotel I indulged myself one evening, and amused the waiter, by skipping the main course entirely. I had a glass of burgundy, french onion soup, a mixed green salad with vinaigrette dressing, a roll without butter, a dry baked potato, and even though I was full after the potato, the temptation of the chocolate mousse was too much. I had coffee *and* the chocolate mousse. It was a delightful, controlled splurge. Eating out can be fun without being fattening.

Another Tip on Successful Dieting

On airplanes, I'm constantly amazed when many of my fellow passengers have almost finished eating before I can unwrap my eating utensils. They seem to inhale their food. Don't make this mistake. Take your time. Savor and chew every bite, completely. Eat slowly and take small bites. You will enjoy your food more and your appetite control mechanism works more effectively to tell you when you are full and satisfied. If you gulp your food down, as many people do, you'll enjoy it less and eat more than you need or want. If you make it a point to take small bites, you automatically eat slower, eat less, and enjoy it more. It helps to use small spoons, forks, bowls, and plates.

Train Correctly

Correct diet *and* correct exercise are required to achieve ultimate muscularity. My diet was near perfection in 1977, but I trained too much and too often. A better training routine would have given me much better results.

I should have known better, I suppose, but like so many others, I got carried away by the bomb-blitz 20 sets per body part routines that many of the champs use to reach contest condition. My 1977 routine was great for reducing body fat and for cardiovascular fitness, but it tore down muscle tissue. I would have maintained more muscle by training less and resting more.

My training in 1977

I trained every day of the week with a six day a week split routine and did up to 20 sets per body part. On the seventh day I rode my ten speed racing bicycle over a 20 mile course. I constantly tried to reduce the time it took me to complete the course and I was finally able to cover the 20 miles in 62 minutes, including time spent stopped at traffic lights.

15

In my frontal thigh routine, I didn't include as many sets as I did for some other body parts, but it illustrates the type of routine I used in 1977. After a warm-up, I did three sets each of leg extensions, hack squats, and leg presses. On each exercise I used the same weight for all three sets, doing as many repetitions as I could on each set. The repetitions were usually 20-17-13. I went through my routine for frontal thighs and for all body parts, with minimum rest between sets. As good as that routine may sound I discovered a flaw in 1979. My strength level in 1979 contrasted to my strength level in 1977 demonstrates my error. In 1977, when I was doing nine sets for frontal thighs and taking no rest days, my best in the leg press was 450 lbs. for 15 repetitions and I was *losing* strength when I peaked at 2.4% body fat. In 1979 I did only *one set* each on leg extensions, leg presses, and hack squats. I trained legs only once every fourth day. The week before the 1979 Past 40 Mr. America contest, I reached a peak of 15 repetitions in the leg press with 650 lbs., a 44% increase over my 1977 best!

Training Results Are Specific

On June 9, 1977, when I had almost reached my goal of fat-free condition, Lovelace Medical Center measured my oxygen uptake capacity. Oxygen uptake is the capacity of the body to utilize oxygen. It is sometimes called "work capacity" and it's the best measure of cardiovascular fitness or endurance. My endurance was 50% above average.* In 1977 I proved that a high degree of cardiovascular fitness can be achieved through weight training. The results of weight training are specific to the type of training system used and my 1977 routine was well suited to achieve superior cardiovascular fitness. In 1978 and 1979 I understood better the relationship between duration of exercise and intensity, and the importance of rest. I learned how to combine diet and training to produce the training effect of ultimate muscularity: maximum muscle with minimum fat!

---

*For more detail on the test, read my article in the November 1977 issue, (Vol. 37, No. 1), of *Iron Man* Magazine.)

PART TWO

Mr. America
Past 40 Short Class

Backstage at the 1978 Past 40 Mr. America Contest.

1978 saw me fat-free:
I wanted to add muscle without fat,
and I learned anabolic steroids can help.
After some rough times,
I said "no" to the low carbohydrate diet
and went back to
my balanced diet of natural foods.

Step Two

My August 24, 1977, body composition test proved I had reduced my body fat to a minimum level; to gain muscle was
obviously the next step. My plan for gaining lean body mass
with a minimum of fat seemed logical enough. I decided to stay
on the same diet of natural unprocessed foods. I continued to
train hard, and increased my consumption of milk, eggs, and
peanut butter. I reasoned that by starting out very lean and
being careful to gain slowly, most of the gain would be lean. Eat
right! Train hard! Gain slow! How could I fail? I didn't fail, but
you'll see there were plenty of stumbling blocks along the way.

The Importance of Keeping Track

Fortunately, right from the start I did some critically important
things correctly. I avoided haphazard methods and maintained
consistent eating and training routines. This made it easier to
detect and correct errors. I carefully monitored my progress so
I was able to pinpoint what worked and what didn't work. Keeping track "forced" me to analyze my successes and my failures.

19

Lovelace Medical Center

Ripped is a direct result of a chance happening in the summer of 1977.

For many years Lovelace Medical Center in Albuquerque, New Mexico, has been involved in aerospace medicine. Much of the research to determine the best conditioning methods for our astronauts has been done by Lovelace. In the summer of 1977 Lovelace was conducting research to determine the best type of physical training to prepare men to tolerate the change from weightlessness in space to the gravitational pull on earth. As a part of that research, the Medical Center was measuring the cardiovascular fitness, or oxygen uptake capacity, of athletes from various sports. Dr. Luft, Head of the Physiology Department at Lovelace, asked if I would agree to be tested as a person whose primary exercise activity is weight training: The test showed my oxygen uptake capacity was 50% above average. Exercise physiologists generally believe weight training does not improve cardiovascular fitness, and Dr. Luft was surprised by my test result. I told Dr. Luft I was planning to enter the Past 40 Mr. America contest in July of the next year and it would be very helpful to my training to know my body fat level. I had been training and dieting for over six months to reduce my body fat to a minimum level: You can appreciate how excited I was at the prospect of seeing the results measured scientifically. The test showed my body fat was a startling 2.4%. Fortunately the outstanding results of those first two tests caused Dr. Luft to take an interest in me and the frequent body composition tests performed on me by Lovelace Medical Center since then form the basis for many of the conclusions I present in this book.*

Hydrostatic Weighing

Since many of my conclusions are based on the results of body composition tests, I want to tell you about underwater weighing, the method used to measure my body composition. The technical term is "hydrostatic weighing."

---

*Lovelace Medical Center was not involved in my use of anabolic steroids.

Physiologists determine the density of the test subject's body by comparing the weight of the body out of water with the weight when submerged underwater. They use a formula based on the density of fat, versus fat free, or lean body mass, to determine what percentage of the body weight is fat. Simply stated, the method is based on the fact fat people can float more easily than skinny people. I've never been able to float! I sink to the bottom like a rock. I vaguely knew that I sink because my body is dense from lifting weights, but my experience with hydrostatic weighing made me understand why I can't float. A lean person is heavier in the water than a fat person of the same weight. As you become leaner and more muscular you become more dense and heavier in relation to the water your body displaces and therefore you sink faster. A fat person floats like an inflated ball and a lean, muscular person sinks like a rock.

Some air remains in the lungs even when you exhale fully and air in the lungs affects the weight of the body under water. In order to insure accuracy, the amount of this "residual air volume" must be measured before the underwater weight is recorded. At the Lovelace Medical Center, I was first sent to the Pulmonary Disease Department, where my residual air volume was measured. It was a complicated, involved procedure which consisted of exhaling and inhaling numerous times into a formidable array of machinery. I asked the lab technician, jokingly, if I would live. Unlike the usual patient, I was obviously quite healthy. With a grin, she said she thought I probably would. This particular measurement of my residual air volume was used for all future tests.

All of the tests began at 8:00 a.m. and I was instructed not to eat breakfast beforehand. They closed off my nostrils with a clamp. Then I took the deepest breath I could and exhaled as fully as possible into a mouth piece connected to a device which measured how much air I could voluntarily push out. For accuracy, this procedure was repeated several times and then the clamp was removed. Next I sat in a metal chair suspended from a scale which gave my body weight in the air. Then I was told to lower myself into the hydrostatic tank and do everything in the water in slow motion, no waves. Rubbing my hands over my body removed any air bubbles which might have collected under my arms and other places. I got into a metal chair suspended in the water from another scale and was lowered until the water came up to my chin. The nose clamp was put back on. I again inhaled as deeply as I could, then slowly exhaled into the same mouth piece until they told me to stop. Remember, they had to know exactly how much air was in my lungs. When they said, "stop," I held my breath and slowly lowered my head under the water and kept it there until they gave me the signal to come up. They recorded my underwater weight while I was fully submerged. They weighed me three times underwater to insure an accurate reading. Once out of the tank, I dried off, dressed, and waited while Dr. Luft and his staff completed the necessary calculations. I was given figures for my gross weight, my fat free weight, and my percentage of body fat.

After repeated testing for two years the procedure became second nature to me. The body composition testing procedure was always exactly the same and my test results never showed any tendency to jump around. I wasn't always happy with the results, but the results never failed to show a logical and consistent pattern. The results have always been confirmed by a hard look in the mirror.

Other Ways to Stay on Course

It's crucial to keep track of your progress. A body composition test will tell you exactly where you stand. I realize many of you are unable to have body composition tests. Progress can be measured in many other ways. You should make every effort to gauge your progress daily because you need constant feedback to tell you whether you are advancing towards your goal. When I visited Arthur Jones, in 1973, I had kidded myself into thinking my condition was better than it was. Don't fall into this trap. Unfortunately I let this happen to me again in 1979. We all want to be better than we are. For most of us it is human nature to see ourselves more as we would like to be seen than as we really are.

I wanted to know if I was achieving my goal of gaining muscle without adding fat. I knew that I must add weight slowly to avoid putting on fat. I decided to limit my weight gains to one pound per month for three months and then have another test to see how I was progressing. As I had done in 1977, I kept a daily record of my weight. My record for the three month period after my first body composition test showed that on August 24, 1977, the date of the first test, I weighed 157 lbs. (Lovelace recorded my weight at 70.6 kilograms or 155 lbs., 11 oz. At Lovelace my weight has consistently been approximately one pound less than my home weight.) On November 15, the date of my second test, I recorded my weight at 160 lbs. I gained exactly three pounds between the first and second weighing. My daily weight record has never failed to produce the weight gain or loss I projected for myself. Adjusting my food intake in accordance with the daily record of my weight, I gained at precisely the rate I had planned. However, the scales don't tell the whole story.

I was a judge at a contest early in 1979 where Mike Mentzer gave an exhibition. From the audience he was asked what he would weigh for the Mr. Olympia contest. He answered, "It doesn't make any difference what I weigh as long as I win!" Mike lost the Mr. Olympia title to Frank Zane by a narrow margin. (After the final posedown, it was Zane 304 and Mentzer 301!) But Mike's answer certainly made the point that monitoring body weight isn't enough. I've learned to use a number of techniques in addition to daily weighing.

Generally, measurements don't mean much, but I *have* found that one measurement is useful to signal fat buildup: I record my waist measurement at the same time I record my daily weight. A real danger sign is an increase in waist size. Waist measurements can be tricky because it's so easy to pull the tape tighter if you don't get the measurement you want. To avoid this, I stand straight, I relax, and I pull the tape at the same snugness each time. I make sure the tape is in place *before* I look down. I resist the temptation to measure a second time if I don't like the reading. If your waist measurement stays up over several days it's time for a correction. A one inch increase in the size of your waist means a big jump in body fat.

A similar monitoring method is the tightness of your pants and your belt. Be conscious of your clothes' fit and don't wait until you can barely fasten your pants before you take action. By then it's too late.

A strength gain also signals a muscle gain. If you are gaining weight, but you're not getting stronger, then you're probably adding fat, not muscle. Don't misinterpret. I'm not saying that if one man can curl more weight than another man he'll also have bigger biceps muscles. Because of leverage and other factors that isn't necessarily true. I *am* saying if *you* increase the amount of weight *you* can curl, you'll necessarily increase the muscle mass of your biceps. But here again, don't kid yourself. You can't cheat heavier weights up and think you're getting stronger and adding muscle. It must be a real strength increase. Increase your poundage, using exactly the same form under exactly the same conditions, before you conclude that you're adding muscle.

Your mirror is the best measure of your progress, but only if you can discipline yourself to see your true reflection, and not what you'd like to see. You must be brutally honest with yourself and if you're not sure you're being honest, then find someone with a good eye, who'll tell you the truth. Pick this person carefully or you may be deceived even more. If your friend tells you only what you want to hear, you're better off without his or her "help."

Another excellent way to judge progress is to take photographs at regular intervals. The problem is good physique photographers are few and far between. If you find a good physique photographer, willing to take pictures of you on a regular basis, you're lucky. A pictorial record of your progress is one of your most valuable aids. It's like time-lapse photography. Changes you may not notice when you look at yourself in the mirror every day are highlighted in the photographic record.

I intentionally left out the caliper or skin fold thickness method of measuring body fat. The proper type of calipers for measuring skin fold thickness must be ordered from a medical supply company and they're expensive. The caliper method is notoriously inaccurate if your fat level is very low. I investigated this method and I rejected it. If you can pinch a roll an inch thick on your waist you don't need calipers to tell you it's time for a change.

Most importantly, always have a goal in mind. You can't measure progress without deciding what you want to progress towards. A goal motivates you and gives direction to your training. I have a realistic short term goal in mind at all times. Without a specific training goal you're like a ship without a compass.

Confusion

My second body composition test was on November 15, 1977, my fortieth birthday. That milestone passed painlessly because of the results of the test. Dr. Luft found I had gained 3.75 lbs. (My home record indicated exactly 3 lbs., but there's always a slight variation between the weight I record from my home scales and the weight recorded at Lovelace Medical Center.)

The gain was: Muscle: 2.54 lbs. (68%)
Fat: 1.21 lbs. (32%)

My fat percentage went up to 3.1%. Dr. Luft said I'd done quite well. At best, he expected my gain to be ⅓ lean and ⅔ fat. Usually when he has his patients gain weight, the weight is all fat. Dr. Luft's patients, however, are usually not exercising while they're gaining.

I had simply continued with my routine of weight training six days per week, and if the weather permitted, I rode my bicycle on the seventh day. The only change was that I ate more, enough to add approximately one pound per month.

I wasn't overjoyed to have added 1.1 lbs. of fat, but Dr. Luft's comments eased my concern. I continued gaining at the rate of one pound per month, increasing my activity level slightly to burn more fat. I added approximately 30 minutes of fast walking on a stationary treadmill after my workouts, because I knew low level exercise (aerobic) causes the body to burn mostly fat. I walked fast enough to increase my heart rate and breathing, but not beyond the point where I could continue to breathe through my nose. Anything faster would be anaerobic work and cause my body to burn mostly carbohydrates, because fat won't supply energy fast enough. Otherwise, I continued as before until February 15, 1978, when Dr. Luft weighed me for the third time. The results were:

Gross gain: 3.09 lbs.
Muscle: .71 lbs. (23%)
Fat: 2.38 lbs. (77%)

My body fat rose to 4.5%. I was disgusted: I had gained almost three pounds of fat! What had I done wrong? Frankly, I didn't know, but I was determined to take off that three pounds of fat.

I suspected I was overtraining and not giving my body enough rest to allow it to add muscle. I continued with my six times per week workouts, but I trained each body part *two* times per week instead of three. I spread my routine so it took three days to train my entire body. Unfortunately, I also began to question my diet. Mistakenly, I followed the herd and increased my protein intake and cut down on carbohydrates. Six weeks later on March 29, 1978, I had lost 3.53 lbs. My body fat was down to 3.8%.

The loss was: Muscle: 2.25 lbs. (64%)
Fat: 1.28 lbs. (36%)

Not only did I fail to lose the planned amount of fat, I lost more than two pounds of precious muscle! I found myself in a frustrating fog.

In retrospect I realize the Incredible Hulk would have had trouble gaining muscle on the routine I was using. Those first few pounds of muscle gain were probably the result of "muscle memory." (Regaining muscle you've had before is aided by "muscle memory." It's easier to replace muscle you've had before, than to put on muscle initially.) I had sacrificed muscle tissue by training like a marathon runner before my first test, and when I added more calories my body put back some of the muscle I had worn off. After that initial gain, I didn't give my body time to do anything more than repair the damage I was doing. The extra calories I consumed to make sure my scales registered a one pound gain every month just built up my storage fat level. The fast walking on the treadmill did burn fat, but at the same time, it reduced the carbohydrates I was burning and they simply replaced the fat I was burning on the treadmill. I *was* on a treadmill going nowhere!

When the third test showed I had lost mostly muscle when I tried to take off fat, it proved what I thought was happening before the first test in 1977. Overtraining made it impossible to hold the muscle I had gained, and actually caused me to *lose* more muscle than fat. Restricting carbohydrates cut my energy supply, forcing a decrease in my workout intensity and promoted an even greater sacrifice of muscle than before.

While it seems clear enough now, at the time, I was extremely confused. If I had not had the body composition tests to make it crystal clear something was drastically wrong, I might still be scratching my head in confusion.

Solution?

I had spent more than seven months trying to gain fat-free weight. My body fat increased from 2.4% to 3.8%. I gained .99 lbs. of muscle *and 2.31 lbs. of fat*. I was getting absolutely nowhere.

Would anabolic steroids help me? I wanted to know.

Anabolic steroids are compounds chemically resembling the male sex hormone, testosterone. They stimulate the utilization of protein by the body. Many athletes believe steroids increase muscle size and strength. The best known steroid used by athletes is Dianabol.

I wasn't sure steroids would help. I'd tried steroids during the 1960's in an effort to increase my total in the Olympic lifts and they hadn't helped then. Frankly, I was skeptical, but as determined as I was to gain fat-free weight, I decided to give steroids another try.

I'm not recommending the use of steroids because I think that's entirely a personal decision you and your doctor make and I make no attempt to justify or condemn the use of steroids. I decided to use steroids and in recounting my efforts to achieve ultimate muscularity in this book, *Ripped* would be incomplete without a discussion of the role steroids played. I want to present *all* the facts as I documented them through my own experience.

Another important fact is that while there's a lot of talk in bodybuilding about steroids, there's very little documented evidence. Because the body composition tests measured my progress both with and without steroids, the tests gathered important information which hasn't been presented before.

To begin without some strong warnings would be irresponsible. Study the available literature on the subject before you make any decision. An awareness of the possible side effects is essential. Two books which have been helpful to me and which I recommend to anyone considering steroid use are, *Anabolic Steroids and Sports* by James E. Wright, Ph.D., and *Steroids: An Adjunctive Aid to Training* by Boyer Coe and Stanley W. Morey, Ph.D. Dr. Wright's book is a balanced review of the scientific research done to determine whether steroids are an aid to strength and muscle development. The book by Boyer Coe and Dr. Morey is the only book I've found which includes comments on specific drugs and dosages for bodybuilding purposes. Both books contain complete discussions of the background, the theory, and the possible side effects of steroid use.*

No one should consider using steroids for bodybuilding purposes before they've reached physical maturity. Steroid use before adult size is reached can cause premature closure of the growth centers in the bones and stunt growth. The continual supervision of a knowledgable and caring physician before, during, and after steroid use, is absolutely indispensable and crucially important.

The Big Gain

I didn't use steroids during 1977. I achieved a body fat level of 2.4% on August 24, 1977, without the aid of drugs of any kind. *Ultimate leanness can be attained without drugs.* Having made that significant point, I'll explain what happened when I took steroids during the six week period from April 1 to May 13, 1978.

---

*Dr. Wright's book is available from Sports Science Consultants, P.O. Box 633, Natick, Massachusetts 01760, $10.95. The Coe-Morey book can be obtained from Boyer Coe, Box 5877, Huntington Beach, CA 92646, $13.00.

I had a file of materials on anabolic steroids which I'd collected over a considerable period of time. I reviewed these materials and then consulted my physician. He prescribed Dura-bolin, Deca-Durabolin, and Anavar, but not without carefully reviewing with me the possible side effects of anabolic steroid drugs and giving me a thorough physical examination, including blood tests. He told me the manufacturers of steroids make no claim that steroids will enhance athletic performance. Many researchers flatly state steroids won't increase muscle size or strength in healthy subjects.

I received an initial "loading dose" injection of 100 mgs. of Durabolin (faster acting than Deca-Durabolin) and then five weekly injections of 50 mgs. of Deca-Durabolin. In addition, I took a 2.5 mg. Anavar tablet with meals three times a day.

These particular drugs were used because their anabolic effect is high in relation to their androgenic effect. Generally, the anabolic effect of a steroid, that is, the promotion of tissue growth or repair, is good, and the androgenic effect, which is stimulation of the male sex characteristics, is bad. The ratio of anabolic to androgenic properties of a steroid is called the "thera-peutic index." The two books I listed earlier contain complete discussions of the therapeutic index of the currently available anabolic steroids. Again, I strongly recommend that anyone considering steroid use read both of these books. Before each weekly injection, I was given an abbreviated physical examina-tion. The blood tests were repeated at the end of the six week period. The physical examinations and the blood tests showed no deviation from normal in any respect. No abnormalities appeared in my physical exams or blood tests during later peri-ods of steroid use.

The manufacturers of anabolic steroids say to achieve ben-eficial results from steroids you must consume adequate amounts of calories and protein. Steroids don't make protein; they allow your body to utilize protein more effectively. I increased my daily intake of calories to slightly over 3000 and my protein intake to approximately 200 grams a day. I restricted my daily carbohydrate intake to approximately 100 grams. My daily diet consisted of:

1 dozen eggs
3 cups milk
3 ounces chicken
2 ounces peanut butter
2 slices bread
1 apple
salad
4 tablespoons yeast
3 tablespoons protein powder
1 ounce wheat germ
bran
vitamin and mineral supplements

I maintained my basic training routine. I worked all body parts two times a week using a six day split routine. My sets per body part were relatively high, approximately nine sets each for lower body parts and twelve or more sets for upper body parts. My repetitions ranged from 8 to 15. I rested only enough between sets to catch my breath. I used the heaviest weights I could. In short, my diet and training were the same as you'd find in any muscle magazine on your local newstand.

As you can see, my diet during this period was quite different than the diet I used in 1977. During 1979 I used neither this diet nor this training routine.

At the end of the six week trial period I called Dr. Luft to arrange for another weighing; I told him I'd gained more than six pounds. He later told me that he fully expected it would be six pounds of fat. Dr. Luft weighed me on May 16, 1978. The results were:

Gross gain: 6.84 lbs.
Muscle gain: 5.43 lbs.
Fat gain: 1.41 lbs.

My body fat percentage increased from 3.8% to 4.5%. Even though I gained four times faster than before, approximately one pound per week versus one pound per month, the gain was 21% *fat and 79% muscle*. In six weeks I gained less than one and one-half pounds of fat and five and one-half times more muscle than I had gained in the preceding seven months. For me, in 1978, steroids made a significant difference. Since normal steroid production decreases as you get older, steroids probably helped me more at 40 years of age, than they would have when I was 25. I hadn't found all the answers, but I felt like the fog was lifting.

Plan for Past 40 America

After the startling May 16 test result, I marked time for several weeks in final preparation for the Past 40 Mr. America contest which was ten weeks away. I wasn't sure what I should do. I *was* sure a number of my competitors would be more heavily muscled, especially in the upper body. I felt equally confident, however, that if I returned to my 1977 fat-free condition, few, if any, of my competitors could match me in the cuts department. This presented a problem. Could I add muscle to my upper body and reduce my body fat at the same time? I had proved I could take off fat, but whether I could do it without losing muscle was a question. I certainly didn't want to lose the muscle I had finally gained. Steroids had allowed me to gain muscle and I had heard they would also help to hold muscle while cutting up for a contest. I settled on a plan, which, with the aid of steroids, I hoped would take off approximately three pounds of fat and add a little muscle to my upper body. By hindsight, the method I chose had its defects, but it succeeded. It also taught me more about the best way to achieve maximum muscle with minimum fat.

The 1978 Diet

Basking in the glow of the May 16 test result, I stuck with the same type of diet: high protein, high fat, and low carbohydrate. I counted calories and grams of protein, but I mainly watched carbohydrates. I kept my carbohydrates to approximately 100 grams per day until five weeks before the contest. With five

31

Five days after the May 16, 1978 body composition test. *Photo by Bill Reynolds.*

weeks to go, I dropped to approximately 70 grams of carbohydrates per day by eliminating milk. Two weeks before the contest, I reduced my carbohydrates to between 40 and 50 grams a day. My daily diet during the last two weeks consisted of:

18 eggs
1 baked potato
1 slice toast
½ apple
vitamin and mineral supplements

It was the same diet that most bodybuilders use before a contest and very unbalanced. I continued to weigh myself daily to see if my weight was dropping slowly. It was! I watched the mirror to see if I was becoming more defined. I was! Everything went just fine except . . .

The Workouts

I strongly suspected I was training too much and too often. I was sure I'd lost muscle as I reduced in 1977, and I did lose more muscle than fat during the reducing period before my March 29, 1978, body composition test. In an attempt to avoid losing muscle, I reduced my sets per body part and cut my workouts down to four days a week. But, I also wanted to add muscle to my upper body. As it turned out, anything I might have gained by reducing my workout days per week was very likely cancelled out by the manner in which I adjusted my workouts to concentrate on my upper body.

I trained on Mondays, Tuesday, Thursdays, and Saturdays. I did no more than four sets per body part, *but* I trained chest and back on all four days. I trained arms three days a week. Calves and thighs, my strong points, I trained two times a week. On Saturdays, I trained my whole body. I remember those workouts vividly. They were long and I forced my body through them, oftentimes, with my hands trembling. I should have realized my trembling hands indicated I was working on nerve and delving too deeply into my reserve capacity.

The Contest

I arranged for a body composition test with Dr. Luft on July 26, 1978, the day before I left for the contest. In ten weeks my body weight dropped 2.65 lbs, but I lost *3.04 lbs. of fat.* I actually gained muscle: .40 lbs. worth. My body fat was 2.7%! The goal I set for myself in May, to lose three pounds of fat and gain muscle, had been fulfilled almost to the ounce.

My mirror confirmed the results of the body composition test. I was as cut as in 1977 and I weighed 7.5 lbs. more. I peaked perfectly. I was ready for the contest.

Still, I didn't know how I would stack up when I stood side by side with the other competitors. I wouldn't know, for sure, how I was doing until the judges called back the finalists for body part awards. I knew things were going well when I was called back as an overall finalist for Best Abdominals, Legs, Chest, Back, and Most Muscular. I won the Short Class, (up to 5 ft. 7 inches), and lost out to former Mr. Universe, Earl Maynard, in the posedown for the overall title. Many people congratulated me and told me how good I looked. My idol of 25 years, Bill Pearl, told me, "I am proud of you." To say I was elated would be an understatement: I was on Cloud Nine!

Dr. Jekyll and Mr. Hyde

In 1978 I learned that for me, at 40 years of age, anabolic steroids are an effective aid for gaining muscle tissue and an aid for holding muscle tissue while losing fat. I learned other lessons from the 1978 season. My trembling hands told me I was overtraining and an incident that occurred in the last week before the contest showed me my diet was wrong.

The effect of a low carbohydrate diet is dramatically illustrated by an incident between my wife, Carol, and I. Carol is my invaluable aid both at the office, (she's a Certified Para-Legal), and at home, (she's a certified super wife!). She seems to understand me before I understand myself and normally we get on quite well. But this day, the effect of my training regimen took its toll. I stayed home from the office and trained in the morn-

5400 GIBSON BOULEVARD, S.E. - ALBUQUERQUE, NEW MEXICO 87108 - PHONE: (505) 842-7000

DEPARTMENT OF PHYSIOLOGY
Phone: (505) 842-7171

July 26, 1978

Clarence R. Bass
305 Sandia Savings Building
400 Gold SW
Albuquerque, NM   87102

Dear Mr. Bass:

The results of the weighing on July 26th were as follows:

Gross Weight:	74.00 kg
Fat:	2.00 kg
Lean Body Mass:	72.00 kg

Since the last test on May 16th you have lost 1.2 kg gross weight and
1.38 kg of fat and gained 0.18 kg lean body mass.

Since the first time we weighed you on August 24, 1977, you have gained
3.40 kg gross weight, of which 0.31 kg (9%) is fat and 3.09 kg (91%) is
lean body mass.

With best wishes,

Sincerely,

Ulrich C. Luft, M.D.
Head, Department of Physiology

UCL/djn

Dr. Luft's letter of July 26, 1978 on changes between August 24, 1977 and
July 26, 1978.

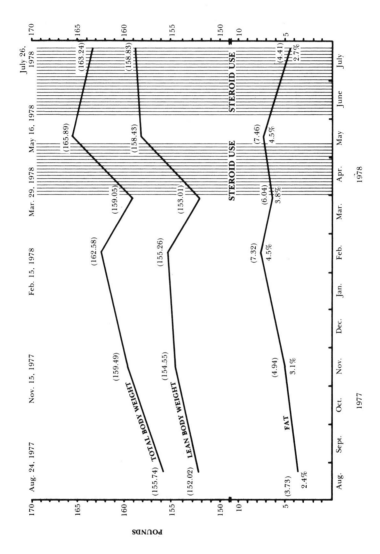

Graph 1. Body composition changes from August 24, 1977 to July 26, 1978.

TABLE 1. CONVERSION FACTOR 1 KG = 2.206 LBS.

Date	Gross Wt.	Lean	Fat	% Fat
Aug. 24, 1977	70.60 Kg	68.91	1.69 Kg	2.4
	155.74 lbs.	152.02 lbs.	3.73 lbs.	
Nov. 15, 1977	72.30/159.49	70.06/154.55	2.24/4.94	3.1
	+1.7 Kg/3.75	+1.15/2.54	+.55/1.21	
		68%	32%	
Feb. 15, 1978	73.70/162.58	70.38/155.26	3.32/7.32	4.5
	+1.4/3.09	+.32/.71	+1.08/2.38	
		23%	77%	
Mar. 29, 1978	72.10/159.05	69.36/153.01	2.74/6.04	3.8
	−1.60/3.53	−1.02/2.25	−.58/1.28	
		64%	36%	
May 16, 1978	75.20/165.89	71.82/158.43	3.38/7.46	4.5
	+3.10/6.84	+2.46/5.43	+.64/1.41	
		79%	21%	
July 26, 1978	74.00/163.24	72.00/158.83	2.00/4.41	2.7
	−1.2/2.65	+.18/.40	−1.38/3.04	
Change Since	+3.40 Kg	+3.09 Kg	+.31 Kg	
Aug. 24, 1977	+7.50 lbs.	+6.82 lbs.	+.68 lbs.	
		91%	9%	

ing. I spent three hours in the hot New Mexico sun putting the final touches on my tan, and *I ate no carbohydrates.* I was more than tired; I was almost in a daze, and even now, I little recall what happened.

Carol tells me when she arrived home from the office, tired from the day's work but looking forward to a dance class we both knew was important to her, I was sitting on the couch in a stupor. I announced I was going out! When she told me I was being unfair (it was my responsibility to take care of our son that night), I showed little concern. I was too tired to think of anyone but myself. It made me angry that Carol was upset. I felt like she was the one who was being unfair. My mental condition bordered on paranoia. I pulled myself up from the chair, grabbed two big nectarines and left the house, completely oblivious of my thoughtlessness. At the time it was an effort to think at all!

Within minutes, the carbohydrates from the nectarines had their effect. I felt like a new person. My body was no longer being forced to work overtime converting fat and protein to provide for my energy needs. The carbohydrates in the nectarines were quickly and easily converted to the glucose (blood sugar) that my brain required to function properly. I left the house an exhausted Mr. Hyde and returned a revived Dr. Jekyll. It's testimony to Carol's commitment to my goals that she understood my predicament. Only after I began writing this book did she remind me of my irrational behavior. All I remember is I felt like hell, and that the rejuvenating effect of the nectarines was almost instantaneous: it was a striking metamorphosis.

My inability to think properly was a direct result of the low carbohydrate diet. If your body and your brain can't function properly on the low carbohydrate diet, then the low carbohydrate diet can't be the best diet for achievement of maximum muscle with minimum fat. By combining overtraining and the low carbohydrate diet as I was doing, and as many bodybuilders do, I was compounding my error.

After the 1978 season I abandoned the low carbohydrate diet. I resolved to make my workouts shorter, less frequent, and more intense. The 1979 season was to test the wisdom of both resolves and teach me further lessons.

PART THREE

Most Muscular Man
Past 40
Mr. U.S.A.

On stage at the 1979 Past 40 Mr. U.S.A. Contest. *Photo by Ken Sprague.*

The lessons of 1979:
steroid use has aftereffects –
bulking up is counterproductive –
short, intense training for best results
and the natural food diet
for the most muscle with the least fat!

Do As I Say Not . . .

I've stressed the best approach is to become lean and stay lean.
I've explained the importance of keeping track of your progress to insure you don't build up storage fat. After the 1978
Past 40 Mr. America contest, I proved what good advice this is,
when I failed to follow my own advice. My demonstration of
the folly of allowing fat to build up while trying to gain muscle
was turned into a disaster by steroids. Steroids doubled the
effect of my foolishness.

The Slump

The purpose of taking anabolic steroids is to promote tissue
growth beyond that allowed by your natural steroid level. When
steroids are introduced into your body artificially, your body
reacts by reducing its normal production of steroids. Your body
registers the increase in steroid or hormone level and by a
feedback process reduces natural hormone production. In short,
your body's hormone producing mechanism gets lazy. Thus a

real problem arises when you stop taking steroids. A delay occurs before your lazy hormone producing mechanism can get going again. When a hormone supply from an outside source is cut off, your body needs an adjustment period. During this lag time your natural hormones are at a lower level than before you started taking steroids. For a time, your ability to build muscle tissue will be less when you stop taking steroids than it was before you started. The technical name for this slump is "metabolic overshoot." My explanation of metabolic overshoot is greatly simplified. For a better understanding of this mechanism I suggest you consult the two books on steroids I recommended in Part Two. The bottom line is, when you stop taking steroids, you'll probably lose all, or part, of the muscle you gained while using steroids.

I was aware of the metabolic lag which occurs after cessation of steroid therapy, but I refused to face the fact I would lose some muscle when I stopped using steroids. I hoped, in some way, I would be immune from metabolic overshoot. This is a common self-delusion shared by many others who have used steroids.

I was *not* immune and I *did* lose muscle when I stopped using steroids. Unfortunately it was February of 1979 before I learned how much effect metabolic overshoot had had on me.

A Losing Proposition

Steroids should not be taken continuously. All pharmaceutical companies recommend that anabolic steroids be taken for a short period followed by a rest period. The length of time steroids can be taken and the necessary rest period before they can be taken again varies depending on the particular steroid being used. Uninterrupted usage might cause the body to shut down hormone production so severely that normal production is permanently impaired. Continuous usage of steroids increases the chance of serious and possibly irreversible side effects.

I stopped taking steroids after the 1978 Past 40 Mr. America contest. My success at the contest really fired me up. I was back in the gym almost immediately. Mistakenly, however, I went forward with my efforts to gain muscular weight. I was determined to add six or seven pounds of muscle by the time of the 1979 contests. I wrote to Dr. Luft about the contest and thanked him and his staff for their interest and help during the past year. I told him I would like to be weighed again in approximately six months. Considering the fact I did not know how much effect metabolic overshoot would have on me, six months was much too long to wait.

Over the next six months I varied my workouts. I made them slightly less frequent and more intense. I trained five or six days a week and rested completely on one or two days. For a time, I trained back and chest three times a week, deltoids, biceps, and triceps two times a week, and thighs and calves only once a week. I finally settled into a six day routine, training all body parts twice a week. I reduced my sets from what I had been doing in late 1977 and early 1978, primarily by cutting back to three or four sets for calves and thighs. I started out training my waist on all six workout days and then cut back to working abs four times a week. I was still overtraining, but the trend was in the right direction.

I stopped counting carbohydrates and went back to my balanced diet of natural, unprocessed foods. I ate just enough to make my body weight climb at the rate of one pound a month. I again used daily weighings and uniform eating habits to control my weight. My training was going well. I knew I was putting on fat, but I felt confident I was adding muscle also.

On February 14, 1979, Dr. Luft weighed me: my body fat was an absolutely awful 9.1%! I was stunned! I wanted to climb in a hole and pull it in after me. Since the last test on July 26, 1978, my gross weight increased 5.96 pounds, exactly as projected. My fat free weight, however, had decreased 5.07 pounds. I had lost 5.07 pounds of muscle and *gained 11.03 pounds of fat!* Still, the full impact of what had happened was yet to come.

Three weighings and four months later, I had lost 9.09 pounds of fat, but in order to do this, I had sacrificed *another* 5.25 pounds of muscle. My body fat was down to 4.1%. I had lost a total of 14.34 pounds. The full impact hit: From July 26, 1978, to June 11, 1979, I had lost a total of 10.32 pounds of muscle!

That ten pound muscle loss hammered home the wisdom of staying lean. Never again will I try to add muscle by bulking up and then reducing down. You shouldn't either. Now the details.

Use It Or Lose It

I was on the spot. I was determined I would be better in 1979 than I had been in 1978. After six months of work, I had lost five pounds of muscle *and* I had over 11 pounds of fat to lose. If I was going to show up at the 1979 Past 40 national contests better than ever before, I'd have to do everything right. My training and diet would have to be as close as possible to perfection.

Exercise physiologists say it's practically impossible to shed a large amount of fat without losing some muscle. If diet alone is used, 75% of the loss will probably be lean tissue. If diet *and* exercise are used a greater portion of the loss will be fat. Exercise protects lean tissue. The use-it-or-lose-it principle comes into play. If muscle tissue is being used, it's much less likely to be lost.

Exercise physiologists have shown through hydrostatic weighing that diet, plus jogging, results in a greater loss of fat and a smaller loss of lean tissue than diet alone. Jogging uses far fewer muscles than a well rounded weight training program. It's a safe assumption that since weight training involves more muscles of the body than jogging, weight training will then protect more lean tissue than jogging. As the intensity of the weight training increases, the amount of muscle being used increases also. My aim was to maximize the intensity of my workouts in order to use as many muscle fibers as possible. I could then protect as much muscle as possible while I lost the 11 pounds of fat.

Four Day Training Cycle

Within a few weeks I settled on the basic workout scheme I used for the balance of the 1979 season. I sifted through the variety of information available from muscle magazines, books

44

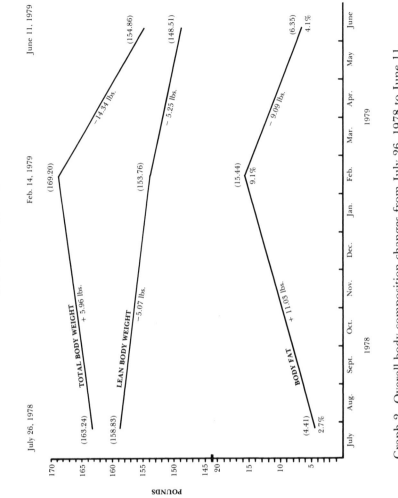

OVERALL BODY COMPOSITION CHANGES
JULY 26, 1978 TO JUNE 11, 1979

Graph 2. Overall body composition changes from July 26, 1978 to June 11, 1979.

on weight training and other types of exercise, bodybuilding seminars, and word of mouth. I combined this information with my own experience. From this conflicting, confusing, and sometimes ludicrous mass, I developed the most sensible routine and techniques for me. And I think, for most people.

I trained my body on a four day cycle:

Day One	*Day Two*	*Day Three*	*Day Four*
traps	calves	upper back	rest
shoulders	lower back	chest	
biceps	frontal thighs	upper abs	
triceps	leg biceps		
lower abs	obliques		

With this routine, each body part receives four days rest before it's directly worked again. I say "directly" worked because there is some overlap between body parts on any split routine. For example, shoulders and arms receive some work when you train upper back and chest. To avoid overlap on consecutive days, I placed my lower body day between the two upper body training days. Using this sequence, upper body parts receive two days rest before being worked again, even indirectly. Legs and lower back receive four days of rest between training sessions. Adequate time is, therefore, allowed for body parts to fully recuperate between training sessions. This is a key consideration: Rest is as important as training. For a body part to grow bigger and stronger adequate rest is necessary after each session.

Equally important is the amount of total body fatigue resulting from each workout session. Your body can become so fatigued from a training session that you can't do justice to the following day's training session, even though the workout involves completely different body parts. By allowing three days to cover all body parts and a fourth day of complete rest, this routine provides time for overall body recovery.

Another factor allowed my body to recover after each workout and helped me avoid excessive overall body fatigue. I did an average of only four sets per body part. Not four sets per exercise for each body part, but a total of four sets for each body part. I never did more than six sets for any body part, and I did as few as one or two sets for some body parts. *This was a major change.* I reduced total sets per workout by more than one-half, which meant that total workout time for each training session was also reduced by approximately one-half. The reduced sets, when taken with the increase from seven to eight days in the time to train the whole body twice, reduced overall weekly training time by *more* than one-half.

All of these changes — four days rest for each body part, no day to day overlap, complete rest every fourth day, an average of four sets or less per body part, and reduced overall workout time — resulted in more intense workouts. With more rest, fewer sets, and shorter workouts, I could make every set count. I was no longer, consciously or unconsciously, forced to hold back on early sets and exercises so I would be able to finish my workout. This workout plan let me go all out on every set of every exercise. It also made my training sessions more satisfying and more interesting. I came away tired, but not exhausted, with a greater sense of accomplishment than ever before. My hands didn't tremble any more.

Intensity

Almost everyone agrees that the key to muscle growth is intensity. Few agree on how to achieve it, however. How many sets? How often? How hard? The school to which the majority of present day bodybuilders subscribe, says that optimum intensity is achieved by doing many sets and even by training twice a day. Undeniably, some magnificent physiques have been built this way; Arnold Schwarzenegger is an excellent example. The other school of thought says optimum intensity is achieved through short, infrequent, and very hard training. Mike Mentzer is both the most outstanding product of this type of training and its most articulate spokesman. I think the Mentzer school makes the most sense because logic and my experience tell me short, infrequent, and very hard training is the best way to provide the muscles with the overload necessary for growth stimulation. Because there are men with the genetic potential to develop mind boggling physiques with almost any system this controversy may never be settled.

My routine is made up mostly of basic exercises. I exclude

some exercises because minor, but chronic, injuries prevent me from doing them. I do no squats or pressing movements only because they aggravate old injuries in my low back and my shoulder, not because I disapprove of squats or pressing. I did squats for years, and if I had to pick one exercise as the most productive, it would be the full squat. Because I do well known basic exercises and because some aspects of my routine are dictated by special problems, I'm not going to list the exercises in my routine. It will be more helpful for me to describe the techniques I use and allow you to adapt them to your own special circumstances.

Proper Set Performance

Increased training intensity starts with correct performance of the basic set. A good set is much more than an exercise done for X number of repetitions. "How much" weight you lift is important, but more important is "how" you lift the weight. You must strive to lift heavier and heavier weights, but not at the expense of proper performance. The keys to proper set performance are:

(1) Concentration (2) Repetition range (3) Form
(4) Effort, and (5) Goals

Concentration

You must concentrate on the exercise you're doing and the muscle involved. If you allow distractions, you won't achieve maximum benefit from a set. Learn to focus your entire attention on the muscle you are working. Put all of your concentration into flexing and extending that muscle. Make the message your brain sends to your muscle a firm command to every muscle fiber to contract and keep contracting until the weight can no longer be lifted. To receive maximum benefit from a set, you must send the strongest possible message to the muscle. You must demand the muscle contract to its utmost on *every* repetition, of *every* set. Concentrate!

Dumbell shrug. Both this picture and the following one were taken in the gym two days after the 1979 past 40 Mr. U.S.A. Contest. *Photo by Bill Reynolds.*

Tricep pushdown, 1979. *Photo by Bill Reynolds.*

Repetition Range

The repetitions in a set should be high enough to fully stimulate the muscle, but not so many that the set ends because of cardiovascular exhaustion rather than muscular exhaustion. I rarely do fewer than six, or more than 15, repetitions.

Generally it takes at least six repetitions to make the muscle really feel worked. My lower repetition limit is based solely on my own feeling. If I fail before I complete six repetitions, my muscles don't feel they've been stimulated enough.

Setting the upper repetition limit at 15 makes sense because, if you do more than 15 repetitions, you are likely to fail when you run out of breath, not because the muscle is too exhausted to continue lifting the weight.

My rule of thumb is if I can't do at least six repetitions, I lower the weight. When I can do 15 repetitions I raise the weight. This varies from exercise to exercise. On upper body exercises, I rarely go over 10 or 12 repetitions. For calves and thighs I sometimes do as many as 15 repetitions, but rarely more.

Form

The form or style of performance should be full range, slow, and controlled.

Full range means from full extension to full flexion. For example, full range motion for the two arm curl is from fully extended arms to fully flexed arms and then back to fully extended arms. This constitutes one full range repetition. To develop a muscle fully, you must work it over its full range of motion.

Perform each repetition *slowly,* insuring the weight is moved through the full range of motion by muscular action alone. If you use a fast style of performance, the weight will be moved through the range of motion partly by momentum. In effect, the weight is thrown up rather than lifted. The muscle works only at the beginning to start the weight moving; momentum, not muscle, is used to complete the repetition. If you jerk or

51

throw the weight up, you'll be using, and therefore developing, only part of the muscle.

Control the weight while lifting it *and* while lowering it. Lowering the weight is just as important as lifting it. The muscle works when the weight is lifted. And it should be made to work while the weight is lowered. More weight can be lowered than lifted and to make the muscle work hard throughout the set you must control the weight more while lowering it than while lifting it. Lowering the weight should take approximately twice as long as lifting it. By controlling the weight throughout each repetition, up and down, you work the muscle throughout the set.

Effort

Your objective is to work the muscle as fully and as hard as possible. This is only accomplished by fully extending and flexing the muscle on each repetition, and by lifting and lowering the weight in a slow, controlled manner.

A good set is complete only when you can't do another repetition in full range, slow, and controlled form. A muscle will grow only when it's called upon to do more than it has done before. To promote growth, continue every set until you think you can't possibly do another repetition. Then do another repetition or two!

Goals

I have a goal in mind with each set. This keeps me progressing. I keep a record of my best recent effort in each exercise. Before each workout, I check to see what I've done before and then I attempt to lift a little more or do another repetition or two. This way I avoid the temptation to stop a set before I reach my limit for that workout.

It's okay to cheat! Once you really have done as many repetitions as you can, in strictest form, cheating allows you to do another repetition or two and make the muscles work still harder. Avoid cheating until it is absolutely necessary, and then, cheat only enough to make another repetition possible and no more. I make a clear dividing line between strict repetitions and loose repetitions. If my best effort with a particular weight is nine repetitions, but I had to cheat a little on the last two, I write down "7 + 2." This tells me exactly what I have to do to reach my goal. I know that to progress I must do eight or more repetitions without cheating.

In addition to proper set performance, I use other techniques to force my muscles to work more intensely. While it may seem masochistic I think most bodybuilders realize in order to progress, they *must* make their sets harder and harder. The harder the set, the better the results.

Heaviest Set First

I do the heaviest set first when my energy level is highest and my muscles are fresh. I warm up by doing a light set or two. Then I go immediately to the heaviest weight I'm going to use in that exercise and I do as many repetitions as I can.

The heaviest set is where maximum overload is applied and it's the set which results in the most benefit. Once the muscle is warmed up and ready for maximum effort, there's no point working up to the heaviest weight with a number of intermediate sets. Medium-intensity, intermediate sets don't challenge the muscle and stimulate growth, but they do reduce the energy that can be put into the heaviest set, the set which does stimulate growth.

It's the last hard repetition, or two, in a set that overloads the muscle and stimulates growth. The same is true of the heaviest set which most bodybuilders do at the end of a series of sets. It's important you note I don't agree with the usual practice. I skip the non-productive sets. I go right to the set that really counts. If I do another set with the same weight and if I have done the first set properly, then fewer repetitions will be possible on the second set. Any time I can equal or exceed the repetitions I did on the last set, I know I didn't do my best on the prior set.

Critics might claim this is a good way to injure yourself. I say this isn't so. The prerequisites are a slow, controlled performance and an adequate warm-up. A jerky, loose performance puts strain on the muscles and joints and can cause injury. For example, a fast bench press which relies on jerk and momentum to lift the weight puts a tremendous strain on the muscles and joints. By contrast, the muscles are worked more thoroughly, with considerably less strain on the muscles and joints, if the weight is lowered *under control,* stopped with *no* bounce at the chest, and then pushed up smoothly, with control. This principle applies to all exercises.

While the second prerequisite, an adequate warm-up, is essential don't overdo it. In an exercise like the leg press, where very large muscles lift very heavy weights, more warm-up is required than in an exercise like the curl, where small muscles and lighter weights are involved. On the leg press, I usually do two or three warm-up sets. On these sets I use successively heavier weights and I hold back to five or six repetitions. These repetitions are just enough to warm up the areas involved, but not enough to tire the muscles and detract from the effort and intensity I can put into the heaviest set or sets. On an exercise like the curl I do only one warm-up set with a medium weight and then I go immediately to the heaviest set. I've never injured myself by using this method. Doing the heaviest and most important set first doesn't produce injuries: It produces better results!

The Descending Set

Because I rarely have a workout partner available to help me I don't use forced repetitions. But I do use the descending set, which, like forced repetitions, allows me to exhaust a muscle beyond normal set failure. With forced repetitions, that is, having someone help just enough to make several more repetitions possible, you continue a set beyond the point where you can't complete another repetition. Your partner doesn't help enough to make additional repetitions easy, just enough to make them barely possible. You "force" a few more repetitions with your training partner's help. The effect is to lighten the weight just enough so you can continue. With the descending set, you achieve the same effect by using a succession of lighter weights.

I often use the descending set technique in the dumbell upright rowing exercise. I line up three pairs of dumbells, the heaviest to lightest. After a warm-up set, I start out with the heaviest dumbells and I do as many repetitions as I can in slow controlled form. When I can no longer lift the heaviest dumbells, I put them down and immediately pick up the next pair and continue to failure again, and then I do the same with the third pair of dumbells. Without stopping, it's three sets done with successively lighter weights.

Usually I do only one three-set series, although I occasionally repeat the procedure after a brief rest. Generally I don't use this technique two workouts in a row on any one exercise. In the second workout, I normally do the exercise with the heaviest dumbells for three sets with rest in between.

When using the descending set technique proper weight selection is important. Muscular exhaustion, not cardiovascular exhaustion should be the limiting factor. I don't want to fail simply because I run out of breath so I keep my total repetitions for the three non-stop sets to about 15. For example, on the first part of the descending set, I might select a weight that will allow six or seven repetitions, a second weight that will allow five or six repetitions, and a last weight that will allow only three to four repetitions. Correctly performed, a descending set makes the muscle feel like it's on fire. The serious bodybuilder understands when I say, "It hurts so good."

I use another technique similar to the descending set on leg extensions. I do as many repetitions as I can, usually about ten, and then I rest for about a three count and do another repetition, then rest again and do another. I continue this "rest/pause" technique for five or six single repetitions. Again, the technique really sets my thighs on fire.

The leg extension is the only exercise where I currently use this version of the rest/pause technique. It can, however, be equally effective when used with other exercises. My experience has proven these various techniques work better for me with some exercises than with others. Once you understand the idea behind the technique, the applications are unlimited. Experiment and see what works best for you.

Modified Pre-Exhaustion

The pre-exhaustion technique is another way to intensify training. Pre-exhaustion involves working a muscle to failure in an isolation movement and proceeding immediately to a compound movement which works the same muscle with other muscles. Examples of pre-exhaustion combinations are leg extensions followed immediately by squats or leg presses, curls followed by palms facing chins, triceps pushdowns followed by dips, dumbell flys followed by the bench press, Nautilus pullovers followed by lat machine pulldowns, and lateral raises followed by presses. The pre-exhaustion technique can be used for almost every body part. The isolation movement exhausts the muscle first. Then by working the pre-exhausted muscle, with other fresh muscles in a compound movement, the muscle is exhausted further than is possible by using either the isolation movement or the compound movement alone.

The pre-exhaustion technique is a valuable tool for increasing exercise intensity, however, in some cases cardiovascular failure comes before muscular failure. You simply run out of breath by doing the compound exercise immediately following the isolation exercise. Advocates of pre-exhaustion say the value is lost if the compound exercise is not done immediately, within a second or two, after the isolation exercise. They claim any further delay allows the isolated muscle to recover and the advantage is lost. I agree: the compound exercise should be done immediately, *if* it can be done without reaching cardiovascular failure before muscular failure. The no delay technique works well for me in the case of the biceps. I can follow curls immediately with palms facing chins and exhaust the biceps without reaching cardiovascular failure. When larger muscles like the thighs, which demand more oxygen, are involved, I usually run out of breath during the compound exercise. My solution is to do the leg extension, rest a full 60 seconds, and then do the leg press. In situations like this, the pre-exhaustion technique works well even with a 60 second delay. My thighs recover to some extent when I rest 60 seconds before the leg press, but I'm convinced the recovery isn't enough to make the pre-exhaustion technique ineffective.

If I do the leg press first, I'm capable of 15 good repetitions with 650 lbs. If I do the leg extension, rest 60 seconds, and then do the leg press, my best effort is 550 lbs. for 15 repetitions. My thighs don't fully recover during the 60 second rest. The 60 second rest not only lets me get my breath, it also allows me necessary time to prepare mentally to exert maximum muscular effort in the leg press. Judging by the burn and the pump in my thighs, this modified pre-exhaustion technique is very effective.

I use pre-exhaustion only every other workout for a particular body part. The technique is mentally demanding and infrequent use keeps my enthusiasm high.

For frontal thighs I do three exercises, the leg extension, the leg press, and the hack squat. Before I start this sequence, I warm up with one light set of leg extensions, and several intermediate sets of five or six repetitions on the leg press. With this preparation I can go through the entire frontal thigh routine without any further warm-up.

On the pre-exhaustion day, I do one set of leg extensions, using the most weight I can, for approximately ten repetitions. At the end of the tenth, or final repetition, I use the rest/pause technique I described earlier. I do five or six additional repetitions with a few seconds rest in between. Then I rest 60 seconds, and then I do the leg press, again, only one set, with the heaviest weight I can handle for approximately 15 repetitions. The leg press completed, I then rest for another 60 seconds. Then I do the hack squat, again one set with all the weight I can handle for up to 15 repetitions. My thighs are exhausted at the end of this three set sequence.

On the alternate day I reverse the order and do the leg press first, the hack squats second, and the leg extension last. Again, I do only one set of each exercise. I don't time my rest periods. To catch my breath, I rest as long as necessary, after the leg press, and after the hack squat. When I do the leg extension after the leg press and hack squat, I have to reduce the poundage for the leg extension by approximately 25% to get ten repetitions. So, it seems doing the compound exercises first also creates a pre-exhaustion.

This is a challenging, exhausting technique but very satisfying. Performing three sets in this manner is more difficult and demanding than doing 20 sets the conventional way. When I've completed these three all-out sets, the leg extension, the leg press, and the hack squat, I know I've really accomplished something! I think you will too.

Negative and Negative Accentuated Sets

In the section on proper set performance, I explained the importance of lowering the weight under control. You can lower more weight than you can lift. Lowering the weight is called eccentric contraction. It's also commonly referred to as the "negative" part of the exercise. The weight is lifted by concentric or "positive" contraction. When you have reached positive failure in a set, you still have a reserve of negative strength. Mike Mentzer has popularized a method for working the muscle to "complete failure" by combining positive repetitions, forced repetitions, and negative repetitions all in one set. Do as many positive repetitions as possible, then with the help of a training partner continue with several more forced repetitions. Finally, your training partner lifts the weight up for you and you continue doing "negative only" repetitions until you can no longer control the weight. In order to use this method with a wide range of exercises you have to have a slave for a training partner. Also, unless you're very careful in your weight selection, you'll run into the problem of cardiovascular failure before muscular failure. I believe the Mentzer method of working the muscle to complete and total failure makes a lot of sense. When practical, I recommend its use though I rarely have a training partner willing to help me on such a large scale. Plus, I prefer to avoid the possibility that cardiovascular capacity rather than muscular capacity will dictate the end of a set. Therefore, I generally use the "negative only" or "negative accentuated" style.

Leg extension. *Photo by Bill Reynolds.*

I do negative only lat machine pulldowns. After a warm-up, I do a regular positive set with the heaviest weight I can handle for approximately ten repetitions. After a brief rest, I increase the weight approximately 50 lbs. I have my training partner help me pull the weight into position and then I lower it in slow, controlled style. On the lowering phase I concentrate on control, allowing approximately five seconds for the bar to move from shoulder level to arms length. This is extremely fatiguing. To do it properly, you must learn to breathe while lowering the weight. If I can control the weight for more than five or six repetitions, I increase the poundage. Combining a positive set to failure, with a negative only set to failure, is very effective. I do another upper back exercise such as one arm dumbell rows or T-Bar rows, but two sets of pulldowns, as I described, is all the pulldowns I find necessary.

I use the "negative accentuated" style on leg curls. I raise the weight with both legs and lower with only one leg. I do one warm up set of regular positive leg curls, with a medium weight for approximately six repetitions, enough to warm up the leg biceps, but not tire them. I then load the leg curl machine with a weight I can lower under control with one leg for approximately seven repetitions. I do one set for each leg. Judging by the feel of the leg biceps, this is the most effective method for performing leg curls that I've found. Generally I do only one negative accentuated set. I use this method every other leg workout. I do leg curls in regular positive style on the other leg day. The lat machine pulldown and the leg curl are the only exercises in which I regularly use the negative or negative accentuated style of performance. But again, the possible applications are many.

Abs and Calves

Most of what I've read about calf and abdominal training falls into the "ludicrous" category. Everybody seems to believe they must train abs and calves every day. In my view this is wrong.

I've tried the conventional every day ab and calf training. I've come to the firm conclusion that abs and calves should be trained like any other body part — hard, briefly, and infrequently. During most of 1979, particularly the several months right before the contests, I did no more than three sets for abs and calves, and I did these sets only twice a week. The result? Best Abs and Best Legs at the Past 40 Mr. U.S.A. Plus, second place in these categories at the Past 40 Mr. America.

Endless sets of ab and calf work are a waste of time and energy. Very likely, these endless sets retard progress. Fat is removed from the waist by dieting, not training. Calves may be stubborn muscles for some people, but like other muscles, in order to grow, they must have rest.

Your objective should be to *develop* the abdominal muscles, not to work them so much the fat will melt away. It won't happen. If you have a layer of fat on your body, your abs will be covered by fat, no matter how many situps, leg raises, and twists you do. To bring out your abdominal muscles, you must do two things: (1), develop the muscles in the abdominal area through intense training and (2), diet the fat off of your whole body so the abdominal muscles will show.

I direct my abdominal training at three areas: upper abs, lower abs, and the sides or obliques. I train *one* of these areas during each training sessions. For upper abs, I do bent knee sit ups on a steep incline holding a dumbell on my chest. In my last training session, before the 1979 Past 40 Mr. America contest, I used a 50 lb. dumbell. I did ten positive repetitions, as many as I could. After I worked my abs to positive failure, I altered the process in order to continue with negative only repetitions. Using my arms, I returned the dumbell, *and then* my body, to the top position. I continued with negative only repetitions until I could no longer control the downward movement, six or seven additional repetitions. I usually repeated this procedure twice. On the second day, I did one set of dumbell sidebends. I used a 125 lb. dumbell for approximately 15 repetitions. I bent to the side until the dumbell touched the side of my foot. I used a slow, controlled style, going down and coming up. I lowered the dumbell at about half the speed I used on the way up. Most bodybuilders don't do dumbell sidebends because they believe they'll over-develop their obliques. My experience proves this isn't so: I haven't developed huge, unsightly obliques and heavy

Photo by Bill Reynolds.

dumbell sidebends are a regular part of my routine. On the third training day I worked lower abs with leg ups on the leg curl machine (see photograph). I did approximately 15 repetitions on the first set, followed by a second set of ten or 11 repetitions. I used as much weight as I could. I rested on the fourth day and repeated the routine. Like other body parts, I trained my entire abdominal area twice every eight days.

Two words describe a properly done set of calf work — "Damned Hard!" For calves, I do very hard sets. Stubborn muscles should be worked harder, not longer. I start out with calves on my leg days so I can really hit them with enthusiasm. First, I warm up by doing toe raises without weight, stretching all the way down and coming all the way up, for approximately 15 or 20 repetitions. I then do toe raises on the standing calf machine with the heaviest weight I can handle for about 12 repetitions. I rest, and then I do a second set with the same weight for as many repetitions as possible, usually nine or ten. I finish with one set on the seated calf machine, with as much weight as I can handle, for up to 15 repetitions. My calves are pumped and tired at the end of these three sets and they require several days to recover. Again, like every other body part I trained calves every fourth day.

These hard, brief, and infrequent ab and calf routines work best for me. I believe they're the best routines for most people.

The 1979 Diet

In 1979, my diet provided the energy for my workouts and still rid my body of over 11 pounds of fat. After my experience in 1978, I wanted no more of the low carbohydrate diet. I went back to the diet I had used so successfully in 1977, but this time I had to use it with more precision. I had to be back to fat-free, ripped condition with as much muscle as possible by contest time.

Within days after the February 14, 1979, body composition test showed my body fat had risen from 2.7% to an alarming 9.1%, the diet I used right through to the 1979 contests was in

Heavy dumbell sidebends. *Photo by Bill Reynolds.*

Leg ups on leg curl machine. *Photo by Bill Reynolds.*

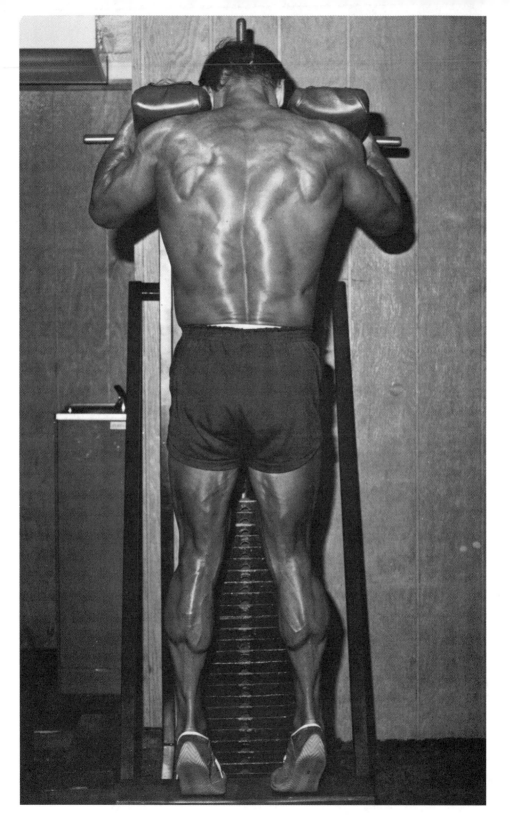

Calf raise. *Photo by Bill Reynolds.*

place. The key calorie control mechanism I used was uniformity. I followed the same basic menu plan every day. I made the necessary adjustments as I went along.

Here is what I ate, and, believe it or not, enjoyed, *every day.* My breakfast was:

2 poached eggs
1 slice whole wheat toast
cereal:
      2 tablespoons wheat germ
      5 tablespoons bran
      1 tablespoon sunflower seeds
      1 tablespoon raisins
      1 cup whole milk

Lunch was the same as in 1977:

1 peanut butter sandwich
1 cup yogurt
1 apple or pear

The bread was the lowest calorie whole wheat I could find at the health food store. The peanut butter contained no sugar or salt, and the yogurt was made from whole raw milk. My evening meal was:

2 poached eggs
1 slice whole wheat toast
huge raw-vegetable salad

The salad was made from various combinations of cabbage, lettuce, celery, tomatoes, cucumbers, squash, green beans, carrots, onions, sprouts, radishes, bell peppers, collard greens, mustard greens, spinach, broccoli, and mushrooms. The dressing was pepper and vinegar, no oil. The limit on the size of the salad was my stomach capacity. I really chowed down on salad. The salad was usually so big and crunchy that it took me approximately 30 minutes to eat it along with my eggs and toast.

About 8 o'clock in the evening I had a liquid mixture: one cup of whole raw milk and one cup of water. For thickening and bulk, I added one tablespoon of Fyblend, a natural fiber supplement from Plus products. Fyblend contains psyllium seed powder, carrot root powder, and cabbage powder. It has no sugar, coloring, flavoring or preservatives. Fyblend is basically tasteless. The milk gives the drink a pleasant flavor, but I usually added one-half grain of saccharin and one-half teaspoon of instant decaffeinated coffee. This is a delightful concoction, with a consistency and taste very similar to an ice cream shake, but it's very low in calories.

I was quite full and satisfied after breakfast and lunch. I was often literally stuffed after my evening meal. That evening shake was delicious. Most important of all, I never felt like a zombie, as I had in 1978. I felt great.

As in 1977, my diet consisted almost entirely of natural unprocessed foods. It was high in fiber and bulk. I ate foods which are large in quantity, but low in calories. *I avoided concentrated calorie foods;* and I lost weight.

At times I tightened my basic diet to lose faster. The most tightening I did was to eliminate the raisins and sunflower seeds from the breakfast cereal, reduce the amount of peanut butter in the sandwich at lunch, and make the evening drink without milk.

This diet is quite satisfying *even at its tightest,* but it does require discipline. Nevertheless, compared to the standard "eat a little less of everything" low calorie diet or the low carbohydrate diet, this diet is an absolute joy. I always felt good and I had plenty of energy for my workouts. I never felt hungry or deprived.

At times I loosened my diet to lose more slowly or to gain. I added a third egg and a second piece of toast to breakfast and to my evening meal. I also had a cup of yogurt with my evening meal and I added a second cup of milk to my mid-evening "shake." This was the highest I ever let the calories go. Even while gaining, I still followed the basic rules, especially: Avoid concentrated calories. When I decided to gain weight, as I did between the 1979 Past 40 Mr. U.S.A. and the Past 40 Mr. America contest, my aim was to gain slowly in order to avoid adding fat. A crash weight gain diet is *never* a good idea.

TABLE 2. 1979 DIET.

Regular	Loose	Tight
Breakfast		
2 poached eggs	3 eggs	2 eggs
1 dry toast	2 toast	1 toast
cereal:	same	same
2 tablespoons wheat germ	same	same
5 tablespoons bran	same	same
1 tablespoon sunflower seeds	same	out
1 tablespoon raisins	same	out
1 cup milk	same	same
Lunch		
peanut butter sandwich	same	reduce peanut butter
1 cup yogurt	same	same
1 apple or pear	same	same
Dinner		
2 poached eggs	3 eggs	2 eggs
1 dry toast	2 toast	1 toast
huge raw-vegtable salad	same	same
dressing: vinegar and pepper	same	same
	1 cup yogurt	
Evening Snack		
liquid mixture:		
1 cup milk	2 cups milk	out
1 cup water	same	same
1 tablespoon Fyblend	same	same
saccharin	same	same
decaffeinated coffee	same	same

One Step At A Time

My long term goal was to peak at contest time. To achieve that goal, many short term goals had to be realized along the way. To stay on course, I used all the tools I discussed earlier: daily weighing and waist measurement, observing strength gain or loss, and the mirror. I used hydrostatic weighing more frequently than ever before.

Guided by these tools, I adjusted my diet as necessary, to move from one short term goal to the next. As I attained each goal I was able to sharpen my focus on the overall goal of lifetime best condition at contest time.

In February of 1979 I knew I had to lose 11 pounds of fat, but what I didn't know, was how much muscle I would lose at the same time. Based on past experience, I assumed that I would lose some muscle no matter how good my diet and training. For my initial goal, I decided to lose five pounds in the eight weeks from February 14 to April 12, when I planned to have Dr. Luft recheck my body fat level. I also set, as a four week goal, the loss of two and ¾ pounds. At the end of four weeks, I had lost three and ½ pounds. I was a little ahead of schedule, but basically right on course. Four weeks later, on April 12, Dr. Luft measured my gross weight loss at 6.95 pounds. The loss was:

Fat: 3.60 lbs. (52%)
Muscle: 3.35 lbs. (48%)

My body fat level dropped from 9.1% to 7.3%. Since I lost approximately one pound per week the result was not bad. In fact, compared to what happened a year earlier, the result was terrific! In the six week period from February 15 to March 29, 1978, I lost 3.53 pounds, roughly one-half pound per week. The loss was:

Fat: 1.28 lbs. (36.%)
Muscle: 2.25 lbs. (64%)

My change from the low carbohydrate reducing diet to a balanced diet of natural unprocessed foods plus the change to shorter, more intense training had their effect. I lost more fat and less muscle. Even though I reduced twice as fast in 1979 as I had in 1978, one pound per week versus one-half pound per week, I lost 16% more fat *and* I retained 16% more muscle — *an overall improvement of 32%.*

In spite of the significant improvement over my 1978 experience, I still had over seven and ½ pounds of fat to lose. If I continued to lose one pound of muscle for every pound of fat, I would lose another seven and ½ pounds of muscle. I couldn't afford to lose seven more pounds of muscle. I had to do something to lose the fat without losing so much muscle. I consulted my physician again and we decided to try a method used by people suffering from illnesses that require them to take steroid medication continuously. My doctor told me some arthritis sufferers have to take steroid medications for years on end. Alternate-day therapy is sometimes recommended for these people. They take the medication one day and allow their body to rest a day before taking it again. Alternate-day therapy often works for these people, and at the same time, lessens the chance that harmful side effects will develop.

Using all the precautions that had been taken in 1978, including blood tests, I took three 2.5 mg. Anavar tablets *every other day* with meals for three weeks. I stopped for a two week rest period. Then I repeated every other day dosage for another three week period. This dosage was less than one-third of the dosage I used during April and part of May in 1978.

With the addition of alternate-day steroid therapy, I continued exactly as before. I used the same diet and the same training routine. I aimed for the same one pound per week weight loss.

On June 11, 1979, eight weeks and four days later, Dr. Luft weighed me again. I lost 7.39 pounds gross. The loss was:

Fat: 5.49 lbs. (74%)
Muscle: 1.90 lbs. (26%)

My body fat was down to 4.1%. With the addition of relatively low-dosage, alternate-day steroid therapy, I lost 22% more fat, (74% versus 52%), and retained 22% more muscle, (48% versus 26%), — a further overall improvement of 44%. For me, at age 41, anabolic steroids had again made a difference. But remember, even with better diet, better training, and low-dosage, alternate-day steroid therapy, I still lost more than one-half pound of muscle for every pound of fat lost. The message is loud and clear. Don't try to add muscle by bulking up and then reducing down. Become lean and *stay lean!*

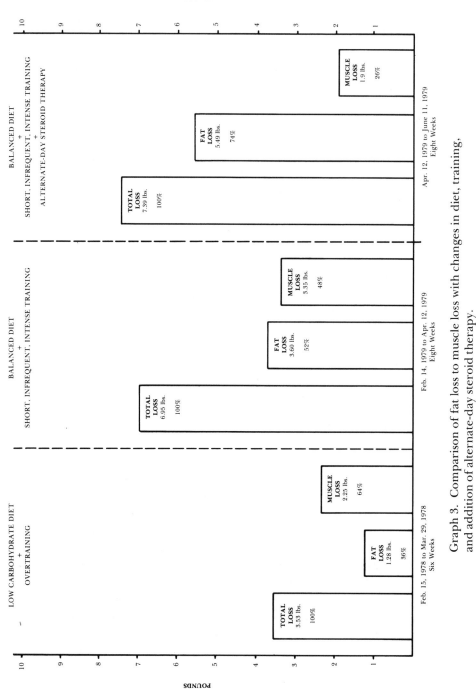

POUNDS

BALANCED DIET
+
SHORT, INFREQUENT, INTENSE TRAINING
+
ALTERNATE-DAY STEROID THERAPY

TOTAL
LOSS
7.39 lbs.

100%

FAT
LOSS
5.49 lbs.

74%

MUSCLE
LOSS
1.9 lbs.

26%

Apr. 12, 1979 to June 11, 1979
Eight Weeks

BALANCED DIET
+
SHORT, INFREQUENT, INTENSE TRAINING

TOTAL
LOSS
6.95 lbs.

100%

FAT
LOSS
3.60 lbs.

52%

MUSCLE
LOSS
3.35 lbs.

48%

Feb. 14, 1979 to Apr. 12, 1979
Eight Weeks

LOW CARBOHYDRATE DIET
+
OVERTRAINING

TOTAL
LOSS
3.53 lbs.

100%

FAT
LOSS
1.28 lbs.

36%

MUSCLE
LOSS
2.25 lbs.

64%

Feb. 15, 1978 to Mar. 29, 1978
Six Weeks

POUNDS

Graph 3. Comparison of fat loss to muscle loss with changes in diet, training, and addition of alternate-day steroid therapy.

BODY COMPOSITION CHANGES
PERIOD COVERED PART III

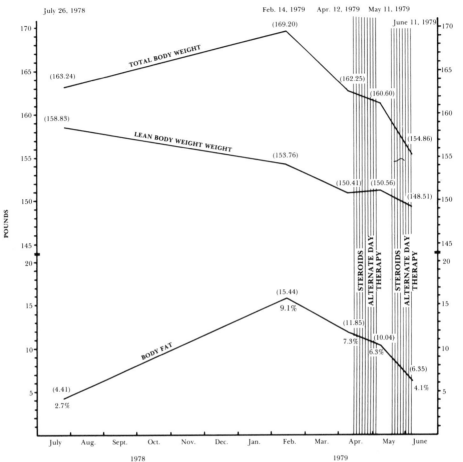

Graph 4. Body composition changes from July 26, 1978 to June 11, 1979.

Fine Tuning the Diet

I entered two national contests in 1979, the Past 40 Mr. U.S.A. on August 4, and the Past 40 Mr. America on September 15. In the three month period between the June 11 body composition test and September 15, I had Dr. Luft measure my body composition six more times to make sure I was headed towards lifetime best condition for both contests. On August 9, the day before I left for the Past 40 Mr. U.S.A. contest, and again on September 13, the day before I left for the Past 40 Mr. America contest, my body fat level was 2.4%. Using the methods and techniques I've detailed, I peaked for both contests exactly as planned. An important, additional factor was the method I used to fine tune my diet in the days immediately before the contests.

By moving from one goal to the next, and checking my progress repeatedly as the contests grew near, I was able to determine what adjustments had to be made to hit the mark precisely for each contest. The last two weeks before the Past 40 Mr. America contest offer a good example of the method I used. I had my body fat checked on August 31, 14 days before the contest. The test showed in order to be at 2.4% body fat for the contest I had to lose approximately two pounds of fat. My body fat was 3.4%. My body contained 5.52 pounds of fat. Reducing my body fat by two pounds, to 3.5 pounds, would put me slightly below 2.4% body fat. With that information, I calculated the necessary dietary adjustments. One pound of fat contains 3,500 calories. Theoretically, to lose two pounds of fat requires a 500 calorie per day reduction for 14 days. Since I was eating the same thing every day, with the aid of a calorie counter book, I determined exactly what foods had to be eliminated to accomplish this calorie reduction. By dropping one egg and one piece of toast from my breakfast I reduced my calories by 175, 100 for the egg and 75 for the toast. I made the same reduction for my evening meal and dropped an additional 175 calories. I was taking two cups of milk in my evening drink at the time. Reducing my evening drink by one cup of milk, 150 calories, I completed the 500 calorie reduction. I failed, however, to allow for one critical factor. Reducing calories by 3,500 will result in a one pound loss *only* if your activity level remains constant.

During the second week before the contest I was spending up to three hours a day in the sun. I lost my one pound all right, actually one and ⅓ pounds, but there was a slight hitch. Dr. Luft checked me again on September 6 and found very little of my loss was fat. Apparently it was mostly water from so much sun. I still needed to lose one and ½ pounds of fat. I analyzed the situation and I saw my miscalculation: I was sweating a lot in the sun, but I wasn't burning as many calories as I would have normally by being active around the house and at the office. My calorie adjustment would have been correct *if* I had kept my activity level constant by counteracting my inactivity in the sun.

I knew what I had to do. I cut an additional egg and toast from breakfast and dinner, (I had been having three eggs and two toast at both meals), and I dropped milk entirely from my evening drink. I did some walking in the evening to make up for the decrease in activity caused by the time I was spending in the sun. When I was checked again, right before leaving for the contest, I was back to 2.4% body fat, and I had learned another lesson.

Without the advantage of the body composition tests right before a contest, I wouldn't attempt to time my peak so close. I would make sure the mirror told me I was ready two weeks or ten days *before* the contest. Then I would hold steady by keeping my diet and activity level constant up to the contest. Even with the aid of the hydrostatic tank, I had to make adjustments the last week before the 1979 Past 40 Mr. America contest. Without the precision offered by the body composition tests, a margin for error is essential. Allow time for adjustment. Don't gamble. Walk on stage at your best!

1979 Wrap Up

It was a very good year. Considering the mistakes I made, the lessons I learned, the obstacles I overcame, and the contest I won, 1979 was my best and most rewarding year. To be able to

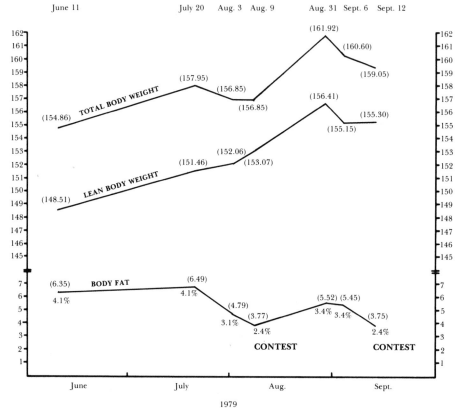

PART III — TESTS JUNE 11 THROUGH SEPT. 15
"FINE TUNING DIET"

Graph 5. Body composition changes from June 11, 1979 to September 15, 1979.

make that statement, at 41 years of age, with over 26 years of deep involvement in the iron game behind me, is extremely gratifying.

The best lessons, the ones that stick, are those you learn through personal experience. I was confronted in February 1979 with an unexpected 11 pounds of fat and I scientifically proved that, in spite of my best efforts, I had to sacrifice five pounds of muscle to lose that fat. I demonstrated, in unforgettable fashion, that to make optimum gains I must stay lean. I would like to have learned that lesson without that giant setback, but without my unfortunate error, I wouldn't have learned so convincingly the superiority of a balanced diet of natural, unprocessed foods, combined with high intensity training, and sufficient rest. I'm proud that with my self-discipline and my determination to win, I came back from what I saw as horrible condition in February 1979 to lifetime best condition in August and the Most Muscular Man award at the Past 40 Mr. U.S.A. contest. I look forward eagerly to the future when I'll spend my time adding muscle, not taking off fat.

LOVELACE MEDICAL CENTER

LOVELACE CLINIC DIVISION
BATAAN HOSPITAL DIVISION
CLINICAL RESEARCH DIVISION
RIDGECREST EXTENDED CARE DIVISION
LOVELACE BATAAN HEALTH PROGRAM

5400 GIBSON BOULEVARD, S.E. - ALBUQUERQUE, NEW MEXICO 87108 - PHONE: (505) 842-7000

DEPARTMENT OF PHYSIOLOGY
Phone: (505) 842-7171

November 2, 1979

Clarence R. Bass
305 Sandia Savings Building
400 Gold SW
Albuquerque, NM   87102

Dear Mr. Bass:

Thank you for your nice letter and the copy of the article which
I read with great interest. I was also pleased to receive that
superb photograph.

I certainly think it is a good idea to publish your experiences so
that other may benefit from them. You are quite welcome to use the
data we obtained on your body composition and I enclose a summary
table with the basic data on all measurements we did this year.
You will also find a reference describing the method we use in
case you wish to include it.

We will be glad to check up on your status some time in December,
as you suggested.

Yours sincerely,

Ulrich C. Luft, M.D.
Head, Department of Physiology

UCL/djn

Enclosures

TABLE 3. BODY COMPOSITION DETERMINATIONS
OF CLARENCE BASS.

Date	Gross Weight kg	Lean Body Mass kg	Fat kg	Fat %
2/14/79	76.70	69.70	7.00	9.1
4/12/79	73.55	68.18	5.37	7.3
5/11/79	72.80	68.25	4.55	6.3
6/11/79	70.20	67.32	2.88	4.1
7/20/79	71.60	68.66	2.94	4.1
8/3/79	71.10	68.93	2.17	3.1
8/9/79	71.10	69.39	1.71	2.4
8/31/79	73.40	70.90	2.50	3.4
9/6/79	72.80	70.33	2.47	3.4
9/12/79	72.10	70.40	1.70	2.4

Method: "Modified Procedures for the Determination of Body Volume by Hydrostatic Weighing". Luft, U.C. and Lim, T.P.K. In: Techniques for Measuring Body Composition. National Academy of Science, National Research Council, Washington, D.C. 1961, page 107.

TABLE 4. CONVERSION FACTOR 1 KG = 2.206 LBS.

Date	Gross Wt.	Lean	Fat	% Fat
Feb. 14, 1979	76.70 Kg 169.20 lbs. +5.96	69.70 Kg 153.76 lbs. −5.07	7.00 Kg 15.44 lb. +11.03	9.1
Apr. 12	73.55/162.25 −3.15/6.95	68.18/150.41 −1.52/3.35 −48%	5.37/11.85 −1.63/3.60 −52%	7.3
May 11	72.80/160.60 −.75/1.65	68.25/150.56 +.07/.15 +9%	4.55/10.04 −.082/1.81 −109%	6.3
June 11	70.20/154.86 −2.60/5.74	67.32/148.51 −.93/2.05 −36%	2.88/6.35 −1.67/3.68 −64%	4.1
July 20	71.60/157.95 +1.40/3.09	68.66/151.46 +1.34/2.96 +96%	2.94/6.49 +.06/.13 +4%	4.1
Aug. 3	71.10/156.85 −.50/1.10	68.93/152.06 +.27/.60 +55%	2.17/4.79 −.77/1.70 −155%	3.1
Aug. 9	71.10/156.85 −	69.39/153.07 +.46/1.01	1.71/3.77 −.46/1.01	2.4
Aug. 31	73.40/161.92 +2.30/5.07	70.90/156.41 +1.51/3.33 +66%	2.50/5.52 +.79/1.74 +34%	3.4
Sept. 6	72.80/160.60 −.60/1.32	70.33/155.15 −.57/1.26 −95%	2.47/5.45 −.03/.07 −5%	3.4
Sept. 12	72.10/159.05 −.70/1.54	70.40/155.30 +.07/.15 +10%	1.70/3.75 −.77/1.70 −110%	2.4
Change Since Feb. 14, 1979	−10.15	+1.54 +15%	−11.69 −115%	

CONCLUSION
The Method Is The Message

I've not given you all the answers for the simple reason, I don't know all the answers. By example, I have, however, recommended a sensible approach which will lead to ultimate muscularity.

Bodybuilding is a thinking man's sport. Frank Zane, Mike Mentzer, and Boyer Coe were not winners in the 1979 Mr. Olympia contest by accident. They succeeded through meticulous attention to every aspect of contest preparation. They came out on top through study, planning, experimentation, and evaluation.

Zane, Mentzer, and Coe are not followers. They would be the first to warn you not to blindly follow the advice of other bodybuilders. A 20 inch arm is not necessarily the badge of bodybuilding expertise. *Listen* to the guy with the 20 inch arm and *pay careful attention* to the ideas of people like Zane, Mentzer, and Coe, but don't accept anything without studying, analyzing, and evaluating it yourself. Success in bodybuilding requires discipline and hard work; but discipline and hard work alone aren't a guarantee of success. You must also use your head. Study! Plan! Experiment! Evaluate! You *will* succeed.

I think that man tries to be better than he thinks he will be. I think that is his immortality, that he wants to be better ... than he thinks he will be and sometimes he's not, but then suddenly to his own astonishment he is.

William Faulkner

Photo by Bill Reynolds.

Photo by Bill Reynolds.

AFTERPIECE
Profiles

As a youth, I toyed with the idea of a career in the iron game, but I was averse to poverty so I chose law school instead. I want to close with a few lines about the people whose influence kept me involved in weight training as an avocation and those who played a major role in creating an audience for *Ripped*.

My Wife

Carol is my partner in more than marriage. She is a partner in my law office, in my workouts, in the writing of this book, and in almost every task I undertake. She knew I was a health nut when we were married eleven years ago, and she's now almost as much of a fanatic as I am. She suffered through the diet and training puzzles with me, and she suffered through the writing of this book with me. Often she helped me find the word or phrase that expressed exactly the nuance I had in mind. I rely on her in almost everything I do. *Ripped* is a better book because of her, and I am a better person because of her.

Peary and Mabel Rader

I've been blessed with the friendship of Peary and Mabel Rader.

I have had the opportunity to weigh the contribution of the Raders to the iron game from many vantage points, including the pages of *Iron Man* magazine, AAU committee work, and dinner conversations. No one cares more about the good of the weight sports, and no one has contributed more than Peary and Mabel Rader.

Since the mid-1950's, when *Iron Man Lifting News* published photographs of me, the Iron Man couple have been largely responsible for publicizing my accomplishments in the weight training field.

In 1969, after the Region Seven Olympic Lift Championships in Alliance, Carol and I shared the Raders' warm hospitality. There've been many meaningful visits since and I've learned much from the Raders. I treasure their friendship and I know all of us in bodybuilding deeply appreciate their contributions.

Bill Pearl

During a training session at Bill Pearl's gym, one of the fellows in the gym told me, "Bill Pearl is a great man." I agree with him. As well as being my physique idol for years, Bill Pearl is an inspiration to many bodybuilders.

Each time I've seen Bill Pearl pose — the 1953 Mr. America contest where he won the title, a thrilling Denver exhibition in the mid-sixties, and his 25 year anniversary exhibition at the 1978 Mr. America contest — I have been amazed by his physique. For years he was the best in the world. And yet, this giant of the bodybuilding world remains as genuine, friendly, and unaffected with his many fans now as he was in 1953. For all the countless autographs he's signed, for each fan, as far as Bill's concerned, it's the first time. Bill told me he wanted to write the most complete, comprehensive book on bodybuilding ever written. He succeeded. His book, *Keys to the Inner Universe*, is a 638-page encyclopedia of bodybuilding. It's a work by a supremely dedicated and knowledgeable man.

Bill Pearl has used his knowledge and experience to help many physique competitors. I knew the area in which I needed the most improvement in the five weeks between the Past 40 Mr. U.S.A. contest and the Past 40 Mr. America contest was posing. I asked Bill if he would help me polish my routine. He willingly obliged. He pointed out the weak spots in my physique, while actually putting me at ease as he did it. I learned more about posing from Bill, in two days, than I learned in two years on my own.

I've served with Bill as a judge; I've been his pupil; and I'm proud to say he's my friend.

Bill Reynolds

Bill Reynolds, in a few short years, has gone from a contributor of photos and articles to muscle magazines, to editor and publisher of his own *Bodybuilding World* newsletter, to Editor-in-Chief of Joe Weider's *Muscle Builder* magazine. If something is going on in bodybuilding, Bill Reynolds knows about it.

Bill Reynolds must like Albuquerque, because he's been here three times in the last two years to announce, judge, and photograph our contests. On a number of occasions he has carried photos of me in the "AAU News" section of *Muscle Builder*. He is always willing to help in any way he can. I particularly appreciate the hours Bill spent taking the excellent photos that appear throughout this book, including the photos on the front and back cover. He's a sensitive man who goes out of his way — who lifts an extra weight for everyone. Thanks Bill! And keep up the good work.

Denie

Denie, Editor-in-Chief of *Muscle Training Illustrated,* is Bill Reynolds' east coast counterpart. Denie was the first to interview and photograph me after my Short Class win at the Past 40 Mr. America. He featured me in *MTI,* carried news items about me, and published my photos a number of times since then. Denie is extremely dedicated to his work. He's determined to see that bodybuilders get a fair shake both within the sport and with the public. I've especially enjoyed the spirited debates we've had through the mail and on the telephone. Denie, you are one of bodybuilding's best ambassadors.

The Weider Brothers

Joe and Ben Weider, above all others, are responsible for the rise of bodybuilding from YMCA basements and beach side shows to the sports pages and television screens of the world.

Ben Weider, starting in 1947, has built the International Federation of Bodybuilders from little more than a glimmer in his eye, to recognition by the General Assembly of International Sports Federations and a membership of over 100 nations.

Joe Weider, "The Master Blaster" himself, has made his *Muscle Builder* the world's most popular muscle magazine. Joe is a superb judge of raw potential. He spotted Arnold Schwarzenegger, whose personality, intelligence, and driving ambition have taken him from stardom in the world of muscle to success in business and acting. Joe continues to find and promote the wonders of nature. As a result, Joe is prospering, the guys with the super genes are thriving, and the sport of bodybuilding is flourishing.

If Ben and Joe had moved things along 20 years sooner my choice between a career in bodybuilding or law would have been more difficult.

OTHER BOOKS BY CLARENCE BASS

THE RIPPED SERIES

Clarence Bass' quest for lifelong leanness begins with the *Ripped series*. Your journey should begin there as well.

In **Ripped**, Clarence explains, step-by-step, how he reduced his body fat to 2.4% and won his class in the Past-40 Mr. America contest. This is the basic diet book for bodybuilders and fitness-minded individuals.

Ripped 2 explains staying lean, aerobics, building muscle, peaking and bodybuilding psychology. Many say it's the best book ever written on weight training.

Ripped 3 contains detailed comments on 22 meal plans that will make and keep you lean. Plus, it's the breakthrough book on periodization training for bodybuilders.

THE LEAN ADVANTAGE SERIES

Do you have questions about losing fat, getting fit, healthy lifestyle, aging or anything relating to diet and exercise?

Chances are the answers are in The Lean Advantage series, where 155 install- ments of Clarence Bass' popular question and answer column, The Ripped De- partment, are collected. Taken together, the three books (The Lean Advantage 1, 2 & 3) constitute an virtual encyclopedia of the bodybuilding and fitness lifestyle.

Here are some of the topics covered: bodyfat tests, successful dieting, muscle building, aerobics, exercise physiology, motivation, preventable diseases, aging and much, much more,

LEAN FOR LIFE

The fitness trend of the new century is balanced training—strength and endurance. Clarence Bass leads the way with *LEAN FOR LIFE*. He explains, day-by-day, how to combine weights and aerobics to achieve total fitness. What's more, he shows how to stay motivated—and lean—forever. He presents a lifestyle approach that will make you lean for life.

> **Don't miss a single step on the road to permanent leanness. Read all of Clarence Bass' books.**

Turn page for more information and where to order.

Also available from
Clarence Bass' RIPPED Enterprises

❖ Posing Trunks

❖ Women's
  Posing Suits

❖ Audio tapes

❖ Videos and DVDs

❖ Color Photos

❖ Food
  Supplements

❖ Selected
  Books

❖ Personal
  Consultations

Model: Dorine Tilton

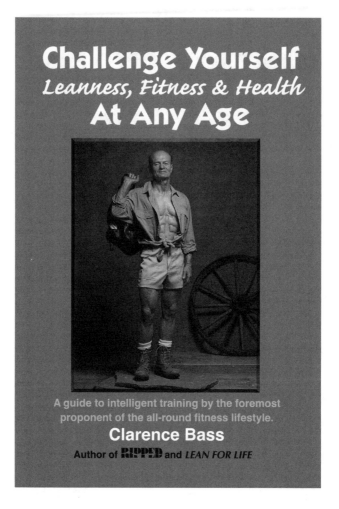

Challenge Yourself
Leanness, Fitness & Health
At Any Age

A guide to intelligent training by the foremost proponent of the all-round fitness lifestyle.

Clarence Bass

Author of **RIPPED** and *LEAN FOR LIFE*

Challenge Yourself is Clarence Bass' latest book. The key to becoming—and staying— lean, fit and healthy is to continually challenge yourself in an intelligent and thoughtful way. That's what this book is about. It explains how Clarence has continued to improve for more than 45 years—and how you can follow suit. The other books get you started and this book will keep you going.

Cutting edge, ***Challenge Yourself*** includes psychologically sound techniques for staying motivated, the latest developments in diet and nutrition, detailed new routines for beginners and intermediates (weights only), Clarence's current routine, athlete-type strength training, high-intensity aerobics, longevity and health topics, and exciting personal profiles.